Text by Denise Jarrett-Macauley
Photography by Peter Barry
Designed by Philip Clucas
Produced by Ted Smart and Gerald Hughes
Editorial Direction by David Gibbon

First published in Great Britain 1984 by Colour Library Books Ltd.
© Illustrations and text: Colour Library Books Ltd.,
    Guildford, Surrey, England.
Display and text filmsetting by Acesetters Ltd.,
    Richmond, Surrey, England.
Colour separations by Llovet S.A., Barcelona, Spain.
Printed and bound in Barcelona, Spain by Rieusset and Gráficas Estella,
Stylist: Sarah Whitelock
Coordination: Hanni Edmonds
ISBN 0 86283 260 8

Acknowledgement
The publishers would like to thank the staff of
Art for Eating for their assistance.

CAKES & CAKE DECORATION

COLOUR LIBRARY BOOKS

Contents

Introduction

Cake decorating is both rewarding and interesting. It is hoped that this book will show how simple it can be and encourage those who use it to improve on their basic skills.

Starting with the simplest icings, such as butter icing, which is easy to use and can create elaborate novelty cakes, the book gradually introduces the more complex techniques required to master the icing and decoration of wedding and other celebration cakes.

Always try to avoid last-minute rushes; many of the decorations can be made in advance and stored. Try to plan ahead when you know that you will be making a special cake and remember that icing and decorating can take time and patience. If you have not had much

practice, start with the simpler designs before trying to tackle a royal-iced celebration cake. You will be anxious that the result should be stunning, so practice first!

Never pipe the design straight onto the cake, as you may ruin the surface you have created. If you are using a complex design, pipe first in white icing then overpipe in colour. This way, if you make a mistake, you have not stained the surface of the cake. The cakes in this book will certainly give you some new ideas and may encourage you to design versions of your own.

Cakes and their decoration is an absorbing hobby. By following and practising some of the designs suggested, it is hoped you will be able to produce a highly professional result – cakes for every occasion.

Lining Cake Tins

All tins must be greased and lined unless you are using a non-stick cake tin, in which case follow the manufacturer's instructions.
If using a shallow tin, only the base needs to be lined for whisked sponges and the quick cake mixture.
If you are making a fruit cake, which will take longer to bake, then the sides as well as the base need lining using a double thickness of greaseproof paper.

To Grease the Tin

Brush with melted lard, margarine or oil. Grease the greaseproof paper with melted fat or oil; if you are using non-stick silicone paper do not grease it. In the preparation of tins, it is necessary to grease and dust them with flour if you are not lining them.

Round Tins

To line a deep, round tin, draw with a pencil round the edge of the cake tin on double thickness greaseproof paper and cut the resulting shape out.
Using a piece of string, measure round the tin. Use another piece of string to measure the height plus 2.5cm (1 inch). Cut out one long strip or two shorter lengths of greaseproof paper to the equivalent of these measurements. If making two lengths, add on a little extra for them to overlap. Make a fold 5mm (¼ inch) deep along one edge and cut into the fold at regular intervals at a slight angle. Place one of the circles of paper in the bottom of the tin, followed by the side pieces and, finally, the second paper circle which will cover the slashed edges.

Square Tins

To line a deep, square tin follow the instructions above for a round tin, but fold the long strips so they fit into the corners of the tin.

Rich Fruit Cake

CAKE SIZES	12cm (5in) round 10cm (4in) square	15cm (6in) round 12cm (5in) square	18cm (7in) round 15cm (6in) square	20cm (8in) round 18cm (7in) square	23cm (9in) round 20cm (8in) square	25cm (10in) round 23cm (9in) square
APPROX COOKING TIME:	2½ hours	2¾ hours	3¼ hours	3¼ hours	4 hours	4¼-4½ hours
OVEN:	140°C/275°F Gas Mark 1	140°C/275°F Gas Mark 1	140°C/275°F Gas Mark 1	140°C/275°F Gas Mark 1	140°C/275°F Gas Mark 1	140°C/275°F Gas Mark 1
Note for all recipes: First ⅔ of cooking time at 150°C/300°F Gas Mark 2						
Butter	65g/2½oz	75g/3oz	125g/4oz	150g/5oz	200g/7oz	250g/9oz
Eggs	2	2	3	4	5	6
Plain flour	75g/3oz	125g/4oz	175g/6oz	200g/7oz	250g/9oz	300g/11oz
Dark soft brown sugar	75g/3oz	90g/3½oz	150g/5oz	175g/6oz	225g/8oz	275g/10oz
Black treacle	½ tblsp	½ tblsp	1 tblsp	1 tblsp	1 tblsp	1 tblsp
Ground almonds	25g/1oz	25g/1oz	40g/1½oz	50g/2oz	65g/2½oz	75g/3oz
Ground mixed spice	½ tsp	½ tsp	¾ tsp	1 tsp	1¼ tsp	1½ tsp
Grated lemon rind	½ lemon	½ lemon	1 lemon	1 lemon	1 lemon	2 lemons
Grated orange rind	½ orange	½ orange	1 orange	1 orange	1 orange	2 oranges
Grated nutmeg	¼ tsp	¼ tsp	¼ tsp	½ tsp	½ tsp	¾ tsp
Chopped almonds	25g/1oz	40g/1½oz	50g/2oz	65g/2½ oz	90g/3½oz	125g/4oz
Currants	150g/5oz	175g/6oz	225g/8oz	275g/10oz	375g/13oz	450g/1lb
Raisins	25g/1oz	50g/2oz	75g/3oz	125g/4oz	150g/5oz	175g/6oz
Sultanas	75g/3oz	125g/4oz	150g/5oz	200g/7oz	250g/9oz	300g/11oz
Chopped mixed peel	25g/1oz	40g/1½oz	50g/2oz	65g/2½oz	90g/3½oz	125g/4oz
Glacé cherries	25g/1oz	40g/1½oz	50g/2oz	65g/2½oz	90g/3½oz	125g/4oz
Orange juice	1 tblsp	1 tblsp	1 tblsp	1 tblsp	2 tblsp	2 tblsp
Brandy	1 tblsp	1 tblsp	1 tblsp	2 tblsp	2 tblsp	3 tblsp

Swiss Roll Tins (Long, Shallow Tins)

Grease and line a shallow tin so that the cake may be easily removed. Line the sides of the tin with paper at least 4cm (1½ inches) longer than the tin, cutting into each corner.

Loaf Tins

When lining a loaf tin the method is again the same, but the paper should be 15cm (6 inches) larger than the top of the tin.

28cm (11in) round 25cm (10in) square	30cm (12in) round 28cm (11in) square
5-5¼ hours	6 hours
140°C/275°F Gas Mark 1	140°C/275°F Gas Mark 1
See note opposite	
300g/11oz	375g/13oz
7	8
400g/14oz	450g/1lb
350g/12oz	400g/14oz
1½ tblsp	2 tblsp
90g/3½oz	125g/4oz
1½ tsp	2 tsp
2 lemons	2 lemons
2 oranges	2 oranges
¾ tsp	1 tsp
150g/5oz	175g/6oz
575g/1¼lb	675g/1½lb
200g/7oz	225g/8oz
375g/13oz	450g/1lb
150g/5oz	175g/6oz
150g/5oz	175g/6oz
3 tblsp	3 tblsp
3 tblsp	4 tblsp

Rich Fruit Cake

This is a traditional recipe which cuts well and is rich, dark and moist. Traditional fruit cake improves with keeping and is used for celebration cakes – weddings, birthdays and Christmas – marzipanned and royal iced. Prepacked dried fruit is ready washed, but if you are buying your fruit loose, rinse it through with cold water and dry it well with kitchen paper or clean cloths. Then spread it out on a tea towel placed on a baking sheet in a warm (not hot) place for 24 hours. Do not use wet fruit in a cake as the fruit will sink.

Mix the sultanas, currants and raisins together. Cut the glacé cherries into quarters, rinse in warm water and dry with kitchen paper. Add the cherries to the fruit together with mixed peel, almonds, and grated orange and lemon rind.

Oiling and lining cake tins.

Sift the flour with a pinch of salt, ground cinnamon and mixed spice. Cream the butter until soft, then add the sugar and cream until light and fluffy (do not overbeat). Add the eggs one at a time, beat well and after each egg add a spoonful of flour. Add the black treacle, orange juice and brandy, if desired. Spread the mixture evenly into a greased and double-lined tin. Use the back of a spoon to make a slight hollow in the centre of the cake so it will be flat when cooked. Tie two thicknesses of brown paper round the tin then bake in the centre of the oven at 150°C, 300°F, Gas Mark 2 (see chart for

the suggested time). With large cakes turn the oven down to 140°C, 275°F, Gas Mark 1, after two-thirds of the cooking time. To test the cake, push a skewer into the centre. It should come out clean if the cake is cooked. When the cake is cooked, remove the tin from the oven and leave the cake in the tin to cool. Turn the cake onto a wire rack and remove the lining paper. Spike the top of the cake with a skewer and spoon a few tablespoons of brandy or other spirit over the top. To store the cake, wrap it in greaseproof paper and foil. If possible, repeat the spooning over of brandy or spirit every few weeks. The cake can be allowed to mature for 2-3 months.

Quick Mix Cake

This is a quick cake, which is ideal for novelty cakes, and the mixture is firm enough to cut into any shape; it is moist and crumbly and can be filled with cream, butter or jam.

Put the margarine, sugar, eggs, sifted flour and baking powder in a bowl. Mix together all the ingredients with either a wooden spoon or electric mixer. Beat for 1-2 minutes until the mixture is smooth and glossy. In a food processor this will take 30 seconds-1 minute. Put the mixture in a prepared tin. Level the top with the back of a spoon and bake in the centre of the oven at 160°C, 325°F, Gas Mark 3 (see chart for the suggested time). When baked, the cake will be firm to the touch and shrink away from the sides of the tin. Loosen the sides of the cake from the tin and leave it to cool on a wire rack. Turn the cake right way up onto another wire rack.

Whisked Sponge Cake

This cake mixture is ideal for afternoon tea and the cake may be filled with cream, butter icing or fruit. It does not keep well and is best eaten the same day it is made, although it can be kept in the freezer for up to 2 months.

Put the eggs and sugar in a

heatproof bowl over a saucepan of hot, not boiling, water. The bowl must not touch the water. Whisk the mixture until it becomes thick enough to leave a trail when lifted. Sift the flour and baking powder together and fold into the egg mixture with a metal spoon, taking care not to knock the air out. Pour the mixture into a prepared tin and gently shake the mixture level. Bake in the centre of the oven (see chart for oven temperature and suggested time). Remove from the tin and cool on a wire rack. When making a Swiss roll, turn out the cake onto a sheet of greaseproof paper sprinkled with caster sugar. Quickly peel off the lining paper and trim the cake edges. Fold and roll the cake up without cracking it. Let it cool a little, then unroll and remove the greaseproof paper. Fill and re-roll the cake.

Madeira Cake

Madeira cake is a moist cake that can be covered with marzipan and then iced with royal icing or any other icing.

PREPARATION TIME: 15 minutes

COOKING TIME: 1 hour 15 minutes to 1 hour 30 minutes

OVEN TEMPERATURE: 160°C, 325°F, Gas Mark 3

175g (6oz) butter
175g (6oz) caster sugar
Grated rind of 1 lemon
3 eggs
225g (8oz) plain flour
7.5ml (1½ tsp) baking powder
30ml (2 tblsp) warm water

Cream the butter and sugar until they are light and fluffy. Beat the eggs in one at a time, then after each egg add a spoonful of flour. Sift in the remaining flour and fold it into the flour with lemon rind and juice. Turn into a prepared cake tin and bake in the oven for 1¼-1½ hours. When cooked, the cake should be firm to the touch. Leave it in the tin to cool for 5-10 minutes, then turn onto a wire rack and remove the lining paper.

Whisked Sponge Cake

CAKE SIZES	2 x 18cm (7in) sandwich tins	20cm (8in) sandwich tin 18cm (7in) square tin	28 x 18cm (11 x 7in) Swiss roll tin	18 sponge drops	20cm (8in) round cake tin	2 x 20cm (8in) sandwich tins
APPROX COOKING TIME:	20-25 minutes	25-30 minutes	10-12 minutes	5-10 minutes	35-40 minutes	20-25 minutes
OVEN:	180°C/350°F Gas Mark 4	180°C/350°F Gas Mark 4	190°C/375°F Gas Mark 5	190°C/375°F Gas Mark 5	180°C/350°F Gas Mark 4	180°C/350°F Gas Mark 4
Eggs (sizes 1-2)	2	2	2	2	3	3
Caster sugar	50g/2oz	50g/2oz	50g/2oz	50g/2oz	75g/3oz	75g/3oz
Plain flour	50g/2oz	50g/2oz	50g/2oz	50g/2oz	75g/3oz	75g/3oz
Baking powder	½ tsp	½ tsp	½ tsp	½ tsp	½ tsp	½ tsp

Quick Mix Cake

CAKE SIZES	2 x 18cm (7in) sandwich tins	18 paper cake cases or patty tins	20cm (8in) sandwich tin 20cm (8in) ring mould 18cm (7in) deep square tin	*900ml (1½ pint) pudding basin *add 25g/1oz cornflour sifted with the flour	About 26 paper cake cases or patty tins	2 x 20cm (8in) sandwich tins
APPROX COOKING TIME:	25-30 minutes	15-20 minutes	35-40 minutes	about 50 minutes	15-20 minutes	30-35 minutes
OVEN:	160°C/325°F Gas Mark 3	160°C/325°F Gas Mark 3	160°C/325°F Gas Mark 3	160°C/325°F Gas Mark 3	160°C/325°F Gas Mark 3	160°C/325°F Gas Mark 3
Soft tub margarine, chilled	100g/4oz	100g/4oz	100g/4oz	100g/4oz	175g/6oz	175g/6oz
Caster sugar	100g/4oz	100g/4oz	100g/4oz	100g/4oz	175g/6oz	175g/6oz
Eggs (sizes 1-2)	2	2	2	2	3	3
Self-raising flour	100g/4oz	100g/4oz	100g/4oz	100g/4oz	175g/6oz	175g/6oz
Baking powder	1 tsp	1 tsp	1 tsp	1 tsp	1½ tsp	1½ tsp
Vanilla essence	4 drops	4 drops	4 drops	4 drops	6 drops	6 drops

For Victoria Sponge see 'Tea Time Treats'.

Variations

Chocolate Victoria Sponge
Replace 25g (1oz) flour with 25g (1oz) sifted cocoa powder. Add this to the other flour.

Coffee Victoria Sponge
Replace the water with coffee essence, or dissolve 10ml (2 tsp) instant coffee powder in 15ml (1 tblsp) boiling water.

Lemon Victoria Sponge
Add the very finely grated rind of 1 lemon.

28 x 18 x 4cm (11 x 7 x 1½in) slab cake	30 x 23cm (12 x 9in) Swiss roll tin
30-35 minutes	12-15 minutes
180°C/350°F Gas Mark 4	200°C/400°F Gas Mark 6
3	3
75g/3oz	75g/3oz
75g/3oz	75g/3oz
½ tsp	½ tsp

23cm (9in) sandwich tin	28 x 18 x 4cm (11 x 7 x 1½in) slab cake; 20cm (8in) round tin; 20cm (8in) square tin	1 litre (2 pint) pudding basin	29 x 21 x 4cm (11½ x 8½ x 1½in) slab cake	23cm (9in) round tin; 23cm (9in) square tin	30 x 25 x 5cm (12 x 10 x 2in) slab cake
about 25 minutes	35-40 minutes	about 1 hour	about 40 minutes	about 1 hour	50-60 minutes
160°C/325°F Gas Mark 3	160°C/325°F Gas Mark 3	160°C/325°F Gas Mark 3	160°C/325°F Gas Mark 3	160°C/325°F Gas Mark 3	160°C/325°F Gas Mark 3
175g/6oz	175g/6oz	175g/6oz	200g/8oz	200g/8oz	275g/10oz
175g/6oz	175g/6oz	175g/6oz	200g/8oz	200g/8oz	275g/10oz
3	3	3	4	4	5
175g/6oz	175g/6oz	175g/6oz	200g/8oz	200g/8oz	275g/10oz
1½ tsp	1½ tsp	1½ tsp	2 tsp	2 tsp	2½ tsp
6 drops	6 drops	6 drops	8 drops	8 drops	10 drops

Basic Icing Recipes and Their Uses

Quick Frosting

This is an easy white frosting which is a quick version of the traditional American frosting. A sugar thermometer is not required for this recipe, but the icing must be used very quickly before it sets.

PREPARATION TIME: 7-10 minutes

1 egg white
150g (6oz) caster sugar
Pinch of salt
30ml (2 tblsp) water
Pinch of cream of tartar

Put all the ingredients into a heatproof bowl and mix. Put the bowl over a pan of simmering hot water and beat the mixture. If possible, use an electric mixer until the icing peaks. Remove the icing from the heat and pour it over the cake, spreading it quickly. This will cover an 18cm (7 inch) cake.

Chocolate Fudge Icing

PREPARATION TIME: 10 minutes

This is a delicious chocolate icing which is quick and easy to make.

50g (2oz) butter
45ml (3 tblsp) milk
250g (8oz) icing sugar, well sifted
30ml (2 tblsp) cocoa powder, sifted

Melt the butter in a small saucepan with the milk. Add the icing sugar and cocoa and beat well until smooth and very glossy. Cool until lukewarm and pour over cake. This is enough to fill and ice the top of a 20cm (8 inch) cake.
NB: if the icing is too thick to pour, reheat gently to thin. This icing can also be made in a small bowl over a pan of gently simmering water.

Sponges: Whisked Sponge, Madeira Cake.

Marzipan or Almond Paste

This is a paste which is made firm and rollable, and is traditionally used as a base cover for fruit cakes before coating with royal icing or any other decorative icing. Prepare the cake by levelling the top, if necessary. Dust a work surface with icing sugar and roll out half the almond paste 2.5cm (1 inch) larger than the top of the cake. Brush the top of the cake with the apricot glaze, or the egg white and brandy. Invert the cake onto the almond paste and, using a palette knife, draw up the top of the almond paste around the cake. Put the top of the cake down on a board and brush the sides of the cake with apricot glaze. Cut two pieces of string or thread, one the height of the cake and the other equal in length to the circumference. Roll out the remaining almond paste into a strip, equal in height and length of circumference of the cake, using the strings as a guide, or cut two short strips of paste instead. Carefully wrap the almond paste round the cake, pressing firmly round the sides and joins. For a square cake, cut the string into four lengths, equal to the sides of the cake and cut the paste to match. Press lightly on the paste when it is placed round the cake in order to produce sharp corners. When covered, leave the cake for 24 hours to dry. Wedding cakes should be left for up to 1 week before icing, otherwise almond oil will stain the icing if the cake is kept after the wedding.

Marzipan or Almond Paste

PREPARATION TIME: 15 minutes

100g (4oz) caster sugar
100g (4oz) icing sugar
200g (8oz) ground almonds
5ml (1 tsp) lemon juice
A few drops almond essence
1 or 2 egg yolks, beaten

Mix the sugars and the ground almonds in a bowl. Make a well in the centre and add the lemon juice, almond essence and egg yolk or yolks to the mixture and form into a pliable dough. Lightly dust the work surface with icing sugar and

Guide to Almond Paste Quantities Required for Cakes

Square	Round	Paste / marzipan
12.5cm (5 inch)	15cm (6 inch)	350g (12oz)
15cm (6 inch)	18cm (7 inch)	550g (1lb 4oz)
18cm (7 inch)	20cm (8 inch)	675g (1½lb)
20cm (8 inch)	23cm (9 inch)	675g (1½lb)
23cm (9 inch)	25cm (10 inch)	900g (2lb)
25cm (10 inch)	28cm (11 inch)	1kg (2¼lb)
28cm (11 inch)	30cm (12 inch)	1.25kg (2½lb)
30cm (12 inch)		1.5kg (3lb)

turn out the dough. Knead until smooth. The marzipan can be stored in a polythene bag or wrapped in foil for 2-3 days before use. Makes 450g (1lb).

Apricot Glaze

PREPARATION TIME: 10 minutes

This glaze can be stored in an airtight container for up to 1 week, if kept in the refrigerator. Re-boil the glaze and cool before applying to the cake.

175-225g (6-8oz) apricot jam
30ml (2 tblsp) water

Put the jam and water in a saucepan and heat until the jam has melted, stirring occasionally. Pour the jam through a sieve and return it to a clean saucepan. Re-boil and simmer until you have a slightly thickened consistency. Cool before applying to the cake.

How to Royal Ice

It does not matter whether you ice the top or the sides first. The important point to remember is that the icing should be applied in several thin coats. Try icing a section first, rather than doing all of it in one go. Your aim is to achieve a smooth surface and you must let each coat dry before applying another. Most cakes require 2 coats on the top and sides, with maybe 3 on the top for a very smooth finish. Wedding cakes require three coats all over and the bottom tiers need 4 coats. For a 2 or 3-tier cake apply 4 coats to the bottom tier; for a 4-tier cake apply 4 coats to the bottom 2 tiers.

Method for Icing a Cake – Icing the Sides of a Round Cake

A flat-sided scraper is essential for

producing smooth sides. Put plenty of icing on the side of the cake and, using a small palette knife, move it back and forth to get a relatively smooth surface and to remove little air pockets. For round cakes, put your arm round the back of the cake and move the scraper forwards on the cake as you can try to get a smooth, sweeping movement without stopping. The scraper should be upright against the side of the cake. Move the scraper off the cake at an angle so the join is not noticeable. If you use a turntable, it will make icing larger cakes easier. Hold the scraper to the side of the cake and use the other hand round the cake so the turntable moves round quickly and smoothly in one revolution. Scrape off any extra icing with a small palette knife. Wipe the cake board and allow each coat to dry for 2-3 hours or overnight before icing the top.

Icing the Top

When icing the base tier of a wedding cake, remember not to add glycerine. Spread the icing on the cake and, using a metal, or firm, plastic, ruler held at a 30° angle, draw it gently across the cake with a positive movement. Try not to press down too hard or the icing will be too thin. Remove any surplus icing from the sides of the cake with a clean palette knife. Leave the icing for at least a day to dry. Remove any rough edges round the joins with clean, fine-graded sandpaper. If the coating is not enough, repeat this 2-3 times. Wait 24 hours before piping decoration onto the cake.

Icing a Square Cake

Ice 2 opposite sides first, then the other 2 sides to produce sharp corners. Hold the palette knife parallel with the side of the cake when icing.

Royal Icing

The consistency of royal icing depends upon its use. For rosettes and flat icing it should be quite firm, whereas for piping latticework and writing it should be a little thinner. When icing is required for any flooding and runouts, it should be thin and smooth. Royal icing can be made in any quantity in the proportion of 1 egg per 225g (8oz) of sieved icing sugar. Keep the icing bowl covered with a damp cloth to keep it moist. As an egg substitute, egg albumen (white) can be bought in specialist cake decoration shops and the instructions for use are given on the packet. The addition of glycerine will aid the softening of the icing when it is dry. This makes it easier to cut.

Wedding Cakes

When icing wedding cakes, do not add glycerine to the two top layers of icing on the bottom tier, so the cake can support the other tiers. Made icing can be stored in an airtight container in a cool atmosphere for 2 days. Before use the stored icing should be stirred well.

Beat the egg whites until frothy with a wire whisk, making sure that the bowl is clean and dry first. Gradually beat in half the icing sugar using a wooden spoon. Beat in the remaining half of the icing sugar with the glycerine and, if using lemon juice, add it now. Beat the mixture thoroughly until smooth and white. Beat in enough icing sugar to give the mixture a consistency which is stiff and stands in peaks. Add the colour, if required. Cover the bowl with a damp cloth and leave the icing to stand for several hours. This allows any air bubbles to rise to the surface of the icing and burst. Before using, stir well with a wooden spoon. Do not overbeat. Note: if you are using an electric mixer, use the slowest speed and leave the icing for 24 hours. It will incorporate more air and will need longer to stand.

Facing page: covering with marzipan, and using apricot glaze.

Guide to Royal Icing Quantities Required to Flat Ice in Two Thin Coats

Square	Round	Icing Sugar
12.5cm (5 inch)	15cm (6 inch)	675g (1½lb)
15cm (6 inch)	18cm (7 inch)	900g (2lb)
18cm (7 inch)	20cm (8 inch)	1.25kg (2½lb)
20cm (8 inch)	23cm (9 inch)	1.5kg (3lb)
23cm (9 inch)	25cm (10 inch)	1.6kg (3½lb)
25cm (10 inch)	28cm (11 inch)	1.6kg (3½lb)
28cm (11 inch)	30cm (12 inch)	2kg (4½lb)
30cm (12 inch)	2kg (4½lb)	

Moulding Icing

PREPARATION TIME: 20 minutes

This is also known as kneaded fondant. It is very easy to use and can be rolled out like pastry. It is ideal for covering novelty cakes and even rich fruit cake. The icing sets and becomes firm. Moulding icing can be used to cover a cake directly or over almond paste or marzipan. If using marzipan first, allow the paste to dry before covering with the icing, which can also be used to make flowers and other decorations.

450g (1lb) icing sugar
1 egg white
50g (2oz) liquid glucose
Food colouring or flavouring, if
* desired*

Sift the icing sugar into a mixing bowl and add the egg white and the liquid glucose to the centre of the sugar. Beat the ingredients with a wooden spoon, gradually incorporating the icing sugar to result in a stiff mixture. Knead the icing until you have a pliable paste. This icing can be stored by placing it into a bag, or wrapping it in cling film, or sealing it in a plastic container and storing it in a cool place for up to 3 days. If adding a colour, sprinkle with a little more sifted icing sugar to keep the icing the same consistency.

To Apply Moulding or Gelatine Icing

Attach the icing by first brushing either the cake with apricot glaze or the marzipan with egg white. Roll out the icing on a surface dusted with icing sugar or cornflour, or between two sheets of dusted polythene. Roll out the icing at least 7.5cm (3 inches) larger than

the top of the cake. Support the icing on a rolling pin and drape it over the cake. Dust your hands with cornflour or icing sugar and rub the surface of the cake, working in circular movements with the palms of your hands to make the icing thinner and ease down the sides of the cake. Smooth out any folds in the icing and cut off the excess. If icing a square cake, mould the corners so that the square keeps it shape. Leave to dry.
NB: liquid glucose is available from chemists.

Gelatine Icing

PREPARATION TIME: 20 minutes

This icing can be used in the same way as moulding icing, but when it dries it becomes quite brittle. The icing can be used to make decorations such as flowers and leaves.

10ml (2 tsp) gelatine powder
30ml (2 tblsp) water to dissolve the
* gelatine*
450g (1lb) icing sugar
1 egg white

Put the gelatine powder into the water, which is contained in a small heatproof basin held over a saucepan of hot water. Stir until the gelatine has dissolved. Sift the icing sugar into another bowl and add the dissolved gelatine and egg white. Stir well until firm, then knead with the fingers until smooth. Dust with extra icing sugar, if necessary. If adding food colouring, sprinkle with more icing sugar to keep the icing to the same consistency. This icing can be stored for 2 to 3 days before use. To do so, wrap it in cling film or a

polythene bag and keep it in a sealed container. If it begins to dry, place or keep the icing in its sealed polythene bag and dip briefly in hot water. Leave for 1 hour and knead well before use.

Glacé Icing

PREPARATION TIME: 10 minutes

Probably the quickest icing to make, it is used on sponges, small cakes and biscuits. To keep the icing liquid, place the bowl over a pan of hot water.

250g (8oz) icing sugar
30ml (2 tblsp) warm water
Various flavourings and colourings

Sift the icing sugar into a mixing bowl and gradually add the water. The icing should be thick enough to coat the back of a spoon when it is withdrawn from the mixture. Add the flavouring and the colouring, if desired. This quantity will ice 18 small cakes and half the amount will ice the top of a 20cm (8 inch) cake.

Variations

Coffee
Replace 15ml (1 tblsp) warm water with 15ml (1 tblsp) coffee essence.

Orange or Lemon
Replace 15ml (1 tblsp) warm water with 15ml (1 tblsp) orange or lemon juice. Add the grated rind of one orange or lemon and a few drops of food colouring.

Chocolate
Sift 45ml (3 tblsp) cocoa powder with the icing sugar.
NB: you must be careful not to keep the icing in too hot a bowl of water, otherwise it will lose its gloss. Also, if a newly-iced cake is moved around without being given a chance to set, the glacé icing could crack and spoil the smooth surface.

Buttercream Icing

This icing is good for covering sponge and quick cake mixture cakes. Butter icing is ideal for covering novelty cakes, as it can be flavoured and coloured easily and is no problem to pipe.

PREPARATION TIME: 10 minutes

125g (4oz) butter
225g (8oz) sifted icing sugar
30ml (2 tblsp) milk
Flavourings (see 'Variations')

Beat the butter and some of the icing sugar until smooth. Add the remaining icing sugar with the milk and flavouring. Beat until creamy. This icing will cover and fill a 20cm (8 inch) sandwich cake. Store in an airtight container in the refrigerator, for several weeks if necessary.

Variations

Lemon or Orange
Add the grated rind of 1 lemon or orange to the butter. Replace the milk with lemon or orange juice. Add a few drops of orange or lemon colouring.

Moulding icing, Royal icing, Butter icing, American frosting and Buttercream icing.

Chocolate
Blend 30ml (2 tblsp) cocoa powder with 30ml (2 tblsp) boiling water. Cool, then add to the mixture with 15ml (1 tblsp) milk.

Coffee
Replace 15ml (1 tblsp) milk with 15ml (1 tblsp) coffee essence.

Crème au Beurre

PREPARATION TIME: 15 minutes

2 egg whites
125g (4oz) icing sugar, sifted
125g (4oz) unsalted butter
Flavourings (see 'Variations')

Place the egg whites and icing sugar in a bowl over a pan of simmering water. Whisk until the mixture holds its shape. Cool. Cream the butter until soft then beat into the egg white mixture, a little at a time. Flavour or colour as required.

Variations

Chocolate
Melt 50g (2oz) plain chocolate in a bowl over a pan of hot water. Cool and beat into the egg white mixture.

Coffee
Add 15ml (1 tblsp) coffee essence to the egg white mixture.

Praline
Gently heat 50g (2oz) of both caster sugar and blanched almonds in a small pan until the sugar turns brown round the nuts. Turn the mixture onto an oiled baking sheet, cool and crush with a rolling pin. Add the 45ml (3 tblsp) of this crushed praline to the egg white mixture.

NB: this icing can be stored in an airtight container in the refrigerator for several weeks.

Confectioner's Custard

PREPARATION TIME: 10-15 minutes

3 egg yolks
50g (2oz) caster sugar
25g (1oz) plain flour
300ml (½ pint) milk
25g (1oz) butter
10ml (1 dsp) sherry

Put the egg yolks and sugar in a bowl and beat until smooth and creamy. Stir in flour and mix well. Heat the milk until hot, but not boiling, and stir into the egg mixture. Return the mixture to the pan and stir, bringing it gently to the boil. Remove from the heat and beat in the butter and the sherry. Pour into a bowl, stirring occasionally to prevent a skin forming. Makes 450ml (¾ pint) of custard.
NB: the custard can be stored in the refrigerator for up to 48 hours.

Basic Equipment and Practising Skills
You will probably have most of the basic pieces of equipment needed for decorating simple cakes: various-sized bowls and basins, measuring jugs, measuring spoons, wooden spoons, spatula, pastry brush, rolling pin, kitchen scales, airtight containers, cocktail sticks, artist's brush and a skewer, to name but a few. However, special icing equipment is often required, so it is wise to invest in a good, basic selection. You can extend your

range as the need arises. Palette knives are ideal for smoothing and spreading icing. They come in various sizes and one would prove most useful. An icing ruler is essential for flat icing the tops of cakes. Choose a firm, not flexible, ruler – at least 30cm (12 inches long, but preferably 36cm (14 inches). An icing rule is even better. An icing turntable is invaluable for icing and decorating large cakes. There are several types of icing scrapers and these are used for pulling round the sides of the cake until it is smooth. Icing cones come into the same category and have serrated teeth of various sizes.

Piping Nozzles

Piping nozzles come in various forms, the metal types giving the best definition. Try to start with a few basic nozzles. The range available starts from size 00. A basic icing-nozzle kit should consist of a fine, a medium and a thick writing nozzle; a shell nozzle; a leaf and a scroll nozzle; a ribbon nozzle (which is also used for basketwork); a forget-me-not and an 8-point and 10-point star nozzle.

Nozzles are available in two styles: plain or screw-on types. Screw-on nozzles are used in conjunction with nylon piping bags and a screw connector. Plain nozzles can be used with paper or nylon icing bags. With this type of nozzle remember that the icing has to be removed in order to change a nozzle. You can either make your own, or use a nylon piping bag or icing pump.

To make a paper icing bag, cut a piece of good quality greaseproof paper or non-stick silicone paper into a 25cm (10 inch) square. Fold in half to form a triangle. Fold the triangle in half to make a yet smaller triangle. Open out the smaller triangle and re-shape into a cone. Turn over the points of the cone so that it stays conical. Secure the join with a little sticky tape. Cut about 1cm (½ inch) off the tip of the bag and push in a nozzle.

Nylon Piping Bags

Nylon bags are sold in various sizes and can be easily filled. These bags are used with a screw connector. The connector is pushed into the bag and protrudes through the hole at the tip of the bag. This allows the nozzle to be placed at the end and secured with a screw-on attachment, allowing the nozzle

to be changed without emptying the piping bag.

Nylon piping bags are most useful for gâteaux as they can be filled with cream, and a meringue nozzle (a large decorative nozzle) can be attached to pipe rosettes.

Icing Pumps

These are bought as part of an icing set; some are made of metal and others of plastic. They consist of a tube with a screw attachment for the screw-on type of nozzle. The icing is controlled with a plunger and is unscrewed to refill the tube. Unfortunately, they are difficult to use for delicate work and you cannot feel the movement of the icing to help control it.

Piping Decorations

Stars

Stars, for example, can be piped with various-shaped nozzles ranging from 5 to 8, or more, points. With the 5-point star, use a nozzle number 13 or 8. These are the most useful sizes. Place the star nozzle in the bag and fill with icing. Hold the bag upright and pipe out enough icing to form a star. Remove the nozzle from the surface of the piped star swiftly. Stars should be fairly flat without a point in the centre.

Rosettes

These are piped with a star nozzle, but using a circular movement. Start at one side of the circle and finish slightly higher than the surface of the icing in the middle of the circle.

Shell

Use either a star nozzle or a special shell nozzle No. 12. Shell nozzles give fatter shells. Hold the icing bag at an angle to the surface on which the shell is required and start piping towards the centre of where the shell will rest. First move the nozzle away from you and then towards you. Push out more icing for the thicker parts of the shell. Link the shells together by starting the second shell over the tail of the first.

Leaves

Use a leaf nozzle, which is No. 10 and has a pointed tip, or sometimes an indentation in the centre of the point. Leaves can be piped straight onto the cake, or on non-stick silicone paper, left to dry

and then placed onto the cake for decoration. When piping you can make two or three overlapping movements to give the leaf some form.

Basket Weaving

See 'Tracy Rose Wedding Cake'.

Templates

These are patterns made of paper or card which are used to transfer the pattern onto the top of a cake. It is easy to create your own or, for simple decorations, i.e. circles and squares, draw round a saucepan lid or plastic storage container. On the 21st birthday cake we use a round template. Draw a circle the size required onto a piece of greaseproof paper and cut it out with a pair of scissors.

Fold the circle in half, into quarters and into eighths, ending with a flattened cone shape. Draw a line in a concave shape from one point to another and cut it out. When the circle is opened, the edge of it will be scallop shaped.

Piped Flowers

Use a large, medium or fine petal nozzle, depending on the size of flower required, and an icing nail, or a piece of waxed paper cut into squares and attached to a cork. Once piped, leave the flowers to dry for at least 1 day before transferring them to a cake.

Rose

Hold the piping bag with the thin part of the nozzle upright. Pipe a cone of icing, twisting the nail quickly through the fingers and thumb. Pipe three, four or five petals round the centre of the rose by curving them outwards.

Forget-me-nots

Pipe these straight onto the cake, using a No. 2 writing nozzle for the petals, by joining five or six dots together round the edge of the piping nail and piping a curved petal in the centre. Alternatively use a forget-me-not nozzle.

Holly Leaves

Colour some marzipan green and roll out onto waxed paper and cut into rectangles. Using an icing nozzle, cut each holly leaf into shape by cutting first two corners of the rectangle and working your way down the sides until you have a holly leaf shape. Mark the 'veins' with a knife point. Roll out a little more marzipan and colour it red for the holly berries.

Christmas Roses

Cover the top of an essence bottle with a little foil and take a piece of moulding icing the size of a pea and dip it into cornflour and roll it into a ball. Shape another piece into a petal (see 'Moulded Roses'). Repeat until you have five petals. Place the small ball in the foil and surround it with the petals, overlapping them. Leave to dry. Remove from the foil and paint the centre yellow with a little food colouring.

Mistletoe

Roll out a little moulding icing, or marzipan, coloured green. Cut into tongue shapes and round the ends. Mark a definite vein down the middle of the leaf with a knife and leave it to dry. Make small, pea-sized balls out of either natural marzipan or white moulding icing.

Moulded Roses

Make a cone with a little coloured, moulded icing and press it out at the base so that it stands. Place a piece of icing the size of a pea in a little cornflour and roll it into a ball. Using a hard-boiled egg, flatten the icing in your hand with quick strokes. Use more cornflour if it gets too sticky. Gently try to get the icing very thin. Carefully wrap the petals round the cone and turn the edges outwards. Repeat the process until a fully shaped rose is achieved. Leave the rose to dry and cut off the base. It may be necessary to use a cocktail stick to curl the petals.

Chocolate Leaves

Break the chocolate into small pieces and place in a bowl over a pan of hot water. Gently heat until the chocolate melts. Do not overheat the chocolate or let any water dilute it. With an artist's small paintbrush, making sure that the chocolate spreads evenly over the surface of the leaf, paint the underside of the freshly-picked, undamaged and washed rose leaf. Allow the chocolate to set and, when hard, carefully peel the leaf away from the chocolate, starting from the tip.

Facing page: a variety of cake decorations.

Novelty Cakes

These are fun cakes enjoyed by all ages, but particularly by children. There follows a variety of designs which can be used for every occasion. It is suggested that you use the quick cake mixture or maderia cake for these. Hopefully this will inspire you to design your own novelty cakes which might be more appropriate for a specific occasion. If you find it difficult to find a cake board for an unusual cake, make your own by covering a sheet of thick card with silver foil.

Birthday Box

30x25x5cm (12x10x2 inch) quick mix cake
Recipe apricot glaze
225g (8oz) marzipan (optional) – this makes the cake a little smoother
Recipe moulding icing
Thin 30x25cm (12x10 inch) cake board or piece of thick card
Food colouring – yellow
225g (8oz) sweets
225g (8oz) royal icing

Egg white, beaten, for attaching moulding icing

Put the cake on a larger cake board. Brush with apricot glaze and cover, if desired, with a thin layer of marzipan. Colour the moulding icing and save 100g (4oz) in a plastic bag. Brush the cake with egg white, roll out the moulding icing and use it to cover the marzipanned cake. With a knife or ruler press lines diagonally into the icing. Roll out the reserved 100g

(4oz) of moulding icing and cover the white side of a thin, rectangular, silver cake board (the same size as the top of the cake). Fit a piping bag with a small star nozzle and fill with royal icing. Pipe shells round the bottom edge of the cake. Put the lid on a basin and pipe shells round the edge of the lid. Decorate the lid with either fresh or piped flowers and a bow secured with royal icing. Place the sweets on top of the cake and put the lid on, leaving them partially revealed.

Clown

450g (1lb) moulding icing
  75g (3oz) coloured pale orange
  175g (6oz) coloured yellow
  150g (5oz) coloured red
  50g (2oz) coloured green
1 large Swiss roll
4 small Swiss rolls
2 sponge fingers (boudoir biscuits)
1 marshmallow
1 recipe apricot glaze
1 recipe royal icing, coloured red

Using the orange moulding icing, break off 2 small rounds and gently flatten them. Make 4 cuts halfway into the balls, to make fingers. Roll out the remaining orange icing into a strip which is 20.5x7.5cm (8x3 inches). Brush the end of the Swiss roll with the apricot glaze and use the orange strip to cover the ends of the Swiss roll. Brush the rest of the Swiss roll with the glaze and with a third of the yellow icing rolled out into a strip 20.5x12.5cm (8x5 inches), cover the glazed area of the Swiss roll. Squeeze the join of the yellow and orange icing so it forms a head and body. Stand the Swiss roll upright on a cake board with something for support. Put the small Swiss rolls lengthways for the legs and brush with glaze. Take a small ball of yellow moulding icing and roll it out into a

This page: Birthday Box.

Facing page: Clown.

10x2.5cm (4x1 inch) width. Divide it into 2 and cut slashes in each halfway up. These will be used for the hair (reserve). Brush the sponge fingers with glaze and cover them with yellow fondant. Stick them with jam onto the sides of the body. Roll out the remaining yellow icing into a strip 20.5x12.5cm (8x5 inches) and cut it down the middle. Use each strip to cover the legs. Roll out a small piece of red icing and mould it over the marshmallow and leave to dry. Roll out 2 pea-sized balls of red icing and use them as buttons. Roll out another small piece of red icing and cut with a pastry cutter. Divide the green icing into two balls, rolling out one and cutting with the same round pastry cutter. Using a cocktail stick, create folds in the circles which radiate from the centre. Work your way round. Cut one of the circles in two and the other into four. Roll out the red icing into an oblong 18x7.5cm (7x3 inches) and attach it to the legs in thin strips. Using the reserved green icing, flatten it a little and cut it into two, shaping each half into an oval. Stick them upright on to the end of the legs as boots. Put half red and half green frills round the neck of the clown, securing them with a little apricot glaze. Put quarter frills round his

wrists and ankles, with a little glaze to attach them to the hands. Secure the hair to his head with glaze. Do the same with the hat. Fill a piping bag fitted with a writing nozzle with the red icing and pipe his features onto his face. Surround him with sweets or put ballons in his hand.

Giant Sandwich Cake

30x25x5cm (12x10x2 inch) quick
* mix cake*
Food colourings – brown, green,
* yellow, pink, red*
Recipe moulding icing
Egg white to brush marzipan
½ x recipe butter cream icing
225g (8oz) marzipan, if required

Cut the cake diagonally so you have 2 triangles. Colour half of the icing pale brown. Divide a further quarter into four and colour the pieces green, yellow, salmon pink and red. Remember to keep icing in a plastic bag when you are not using it to prevent it drying out. For the lettuce, roll out an irregular shape with the green icing and crinkle it up using a cocktail stick so it looks like ruched material. Reserve on a sheet of non-stick silicone paper. To make the ham, roll out the pink icing with a pinch of white icing, making sure the colours stay separate. Roll out into an oval shape and reserve. For the cheese, roll the yellow icing into a 10cm (4 inch) square and reserve. For the tomato slices, roll the red icing into a 10cm (4 inch) square and with a small, plain round

pastry cutter cut rounds. Roll out the pale brown icing into 6 strips all 5cm (2 inches) wide: two 30cm (12 inches) long, two 25cm (10 inches) long, two 40cm (16 inches) long. Use the egg white and brush the sides of the triangles. Stick the brown strips onto the appropriate length sides. The longest strips go along the cut diagonally. Roll out the remaining white icing into a triangle large enough to cover the top of one triangular cake piece. Brush the top of the cake triangle and fix on the moulding icing triangle. Spread the top of the other cake, the one without white moulding icing, with a little butter icing to make the bottom half of the sandwich and make sure it is on either a presentation plate or a cake board. Round the edges of the bottom triangle lay the lettuce, ham, tomato and cheese so they spill out of the cake. Sandwich together with the iced triangle. Fit a piping bag with a star nozzle and fill with the remaining butter icing. Pipe irregular swirls in between the lettuce, tomato, cheese and ham. Dust the top of the triangular cake with a little icing sugar.

Birthday Breakfast

Rich fruit cake (measure the size of
* your frying pan and bake a cake*
* that will fit)*
Recipe apricot glaze
100g (4oz) white moulding icing
Food colourings – brown, pink
425g (15oz) tin apricot halves

Transfer the fruit cake to the frying pan. Brush the top with apricot glaze. Roll out the white moulding icing and cut into several irregular shapes, rounding off any sharp corners. Roll the remaining icing into sausage shapes and brush them with a little brown and pink food colouring. Drain the tin of apricot halves. Place the irregular white moulding icing shapes on top of the cake, putting an inverted apricot half on each one. Put the sausages in the pan. Brush the sausages and the apricot halves with a little apricot glaze.

Giant Sandwich Cake (top left) and Birthday Breakfast (bottom left).

Camelot Castle

20cm (8 inch) square 6-egg Victoria
* sponge*
Recipe butter cream icing
Recipe apricot glaze
4 ice-cream cones
4 miniature Swiss rolls
1 rectangular plain biscuit
1 water biscuit
100g (4oz) granulated sugar
100g (4oz) moulding icing
Recipe royal icing
Sugar flowers
Silver balls
3 or 4 small sandwich flags
Food colourings – pink, green, red

Toffee Water (To Fill Moat)
225g (8oz) granulated sugar
150ml (5 fl oz) water
Blue food colouring
Sugar thermometer, if available

Cut a 5cm (2 inch) wide slice from a cake. Put the other cake towards the back of the cake board. Sandwich the large section of cake to the cake on the board with some butter icing. Make sure it sits towards the back of the base cake. With apricot glaze, secure the 5cm (2 inch) slice on the front edge of the cake board. Using apricot glaze, brush the ends of the small Swiss rolls and place them in the four corners of the cake, placing the ice-cream cones on top. Cover the small Swiss rolls, ice-cream cones and the top and sides of the cake with butter icing. Also ice the 5cm (2 inch) slice. Put the water biscuit on the front side of the cake between the 2 Swiss roll towers. Put the granulated sugar, with a few drops of pink food colouring, in a bowl and stir well until the sugar takes up the colour. Sprinkle the coloured sugar over the ice-cream cones, the top of the castle and the grounds. Fit a star nozzle to a piping bag and fill with royal icing. Pipe round the top of the castle walls and over the front surface of the water biscuit. When the piped stars are just drying, go round the top of the walls and pipe another row of stars on top of each alternate star. Put a silver ball in the centre of each of the stars round the edge of the door and 2 for doorknobs. Colour a little of the royal icing green, and a little red, and pipe the green vine with red stars for flowers. You can also use sugar flowers.

To Make the Water to Fill the Moat
Colour the moulding icing green and roll it out to form a long sausage which will go round the

shortest ends with pinking shears or cut with a pastry wheel. With a little water attach the ribbons of fondant to the inside of the shoes approximately halfway between the toe and heel. With a cocktail stick, gently mark round the top of the shoe, then the sole. Cut two 15cm (6 inch) long, string-width strips of fondant and make a little bow out of each and put them in place. As an alternative, pink satin ribbon can be used in place of fondant. Fill the shoes with sweets.

Football Boot

25x20cm (10x8 inch) quick mix cake
Jam for filling
Recipe apricot glaze
Recipe moulding icing
Recipe butter icing
50g (2oz) desiccated coconut
50g (2oz) chocolate dots
Food colouring – red, yellow, black and green
Medium star nozzle and piping bag
2 liquorice laces
30cm (12 inch) square cake board
1 cocktail stick

Cut the cake horizontally and sandwich with jam for filling. Put the cakes on the board. With a cocktail stick mark out the outline of the boot. When you are happy with the outline, cut it out with a sharp knife and brush with apricot glaze. Divide the moulding icing into two, remembering to keep the icing in a plastic bag when not in use. Roll out half the icing into an oblong and cover the boot shape (top and sides). Do not ice the leg. Cut the icing at the ankle to indicate the top of the boot. Divide the remaining icing into two, colouring half red and the rest yellow. Draw out the shapes for the patches, tongue of the boot and the flash on some greaseproof paper. Draw a large 'E' with a double line and cut it out. This should be used as a template to guide you when you roll out the red icing to cover the ankle and the

edge of the board. Use the icing to form a wall and stick it down by smoothing it onto the board, then leave it to dry for one hour. Heat the sugar and water so the sugar dissolves and boils. Continue to boil the mixture until it reaches 'soft crack' point, that is, just before it starts to colour. If a sugar thermometer is available, the reading should be 132-143°C, 270-290°F. Pour the sugar mixture into the moat. Put the sugar flowers on the green banks of the moat and lay the biscuit across from the castle to the land to form a drawbridge. Use the flags to decorate.

Ballet Shoes

2 Swiss rolls
30cm (12 inch) square cake board
900g (2lb) fondant icing
Food colouring – pink
Recipe apricot glaze
Cornflour to dust
60ml (4 tblsp) jam
1 metre (1 yard) pink satin ribbon (as an alternative to fondant ribbons)

To Make Shoes

Cut the edge of one end of the cake into a point. Then cut the tip of the point. This will be the toe end of the shoe. Repeat for the

other shoe and place them both on the cake board. Cut the other end of the cake, rounding it slightly. Cut out a long oval towards the heel end of the cake. Press the cake in firmly, but gently, to create an instep. Colour all the fondant pale pink. Brush the cake with the glaze. Roll out the fondant on the cornflour-dusted work surface. Press the fondant down and smooth out any cracks. Mould it gently round the toe and take special care to squeeze and tuck it into the inside of the shoe. Cut off any excess and re-mould it into a ball. Roll out. Cut 4 long strips 2.5cm (1 inch) wide and cut the

This page: Camelot Castle.

Facing page: Ballet Shoes (top) and Football Boot (bottom).

flash for the side of the boot. Roll out the yellow moulding icing and cut the same shapes, but smaller, to go on top of the red. Cut the liquorice laces and tie into a bow. With a little icing place it at the ankle. Mix half of the butter icing yellow and half red. Fill a piping bag with the red butter icing and pipe a band about 6 stripes wide, then repeat with the yellow icing. Work your way up the leg until you have 3 red bands and 2 yellow. Put rows of chocolate drops on the side of the boot to represent studs. Put the desiccated coconut in a bowl and add a few drops of green food colour. Stir in and use to sprinkle on the board to represent grass.

Shirt and Tie

13x9x2cm (15x3½x¾ inch) quick
  mix cake
2 x recipe butter cream icing
100g (4oz) coloured fondant, if using
  design with tie
1 small packet round sweets, e.g.
  jellies, fruit gums or milk drops
Food colouring – red

In a clean bowl reserve ¼ of the butter cream icing and with the food colouring make up a darker shade of the colour previously used. Wash the tin used for baking the cake and, if the tin is old or marked, line with foil so that the tin is totally covered both inside and out. You could otherwise find or make an old shirt box. Put the cake into the cake tin or box, and spread with the lighter icing. If the cake fits snugly into its box or tin, only ice the top; if not, ice all the visible cake. Make the neck and collar shaping by first marking it out. Draw a line in the icing with a cocktail stick 7.5cm (3 inches) from one end of the cake. (The 23cm (9 inch) sides are top and bottom). This marks the shoulder line, so use this line to guide you when building up the collar with more icing. Half the collar (front and back) should be on either side of the faint line. Fill the piping bag with the darker icing and with a writing nozzle outline the collar and shoulder seam. Roll out a thin strip of fondant 4cm (1½ inches) wide and 35cm (14 inches) long, pinch it in to form the knot and place on the cake. If you are using the design with centre placket (shirt front) pocket and sleeves use the darker icing in the piping bag and pipe the shirt front, pocket and sleeves. Put the sweets in position as buttons.

Artist's Palette

23cm (9 inch) square quick mix cake
Recipe apricot glaze
350g (¾lb) moulding icing
100g (4oz) granulated sugar
Food colourings – red, blue, green,
  yellow, orange, violet and brown

Cut a kidney shape out of the cake and carefully cut a circle slightly off centre. Place the cake on the cake board and brush with apricot glaze. Colour all except 50g (2oz) of the moulding icing pale brown. Roll out and use to cover the palette, pushing in gently at the hole so that the icing coats the inner wall of the circle. Push down to reveal the cake board. Using a dry brush, dip gently into the brown food colouring and drag hesitantly across the palette. Wipe the brush with kitchen paper to absorb some of the food colouring and continue to cover the palette with the wood grain. Leave to dry. Colour 15ml (1 tblsp) of granulated sugar with each of the food colourings. This is done by adding a few drops and stirring until the sugar absorbs the colour. Roll out the remaining moulding icing into a long sausage shape and cut into half. Make a point at the end of one sausage and leave to dry and gently flatten the end of the other.

To Make the Pencil and Paintbrush
When the moulding icing shapes are dry, copying a pencil, colour the one with the pointed end by painting in the lead and the outside. Copy the brush you are using and place them next to the palette. When the palette is dry, put little mounds of the coloured sugar on the top.

Pugwash at Sea

29x21x4cm (11½x8½x1½ inch)
  quick mix cake
Recipe royal icing
Recipe butter icing
225g (8oz) moulding icing
Recipe apricot glaze
1 packet of mints with a hole
1 black liquorice sweet
1 sandwich flag
Food colourings – including blue

Cut a 10cm (4 inch) slice from the shortest side of the cake. From the smallest cake cut 5cm (2 inch) slice from one end. Cut a point out of the remaining rectangle measuring 16.5x10cm (6½x4 inches). Place

Artist's Palette (left) and Shirt and Tie (below).

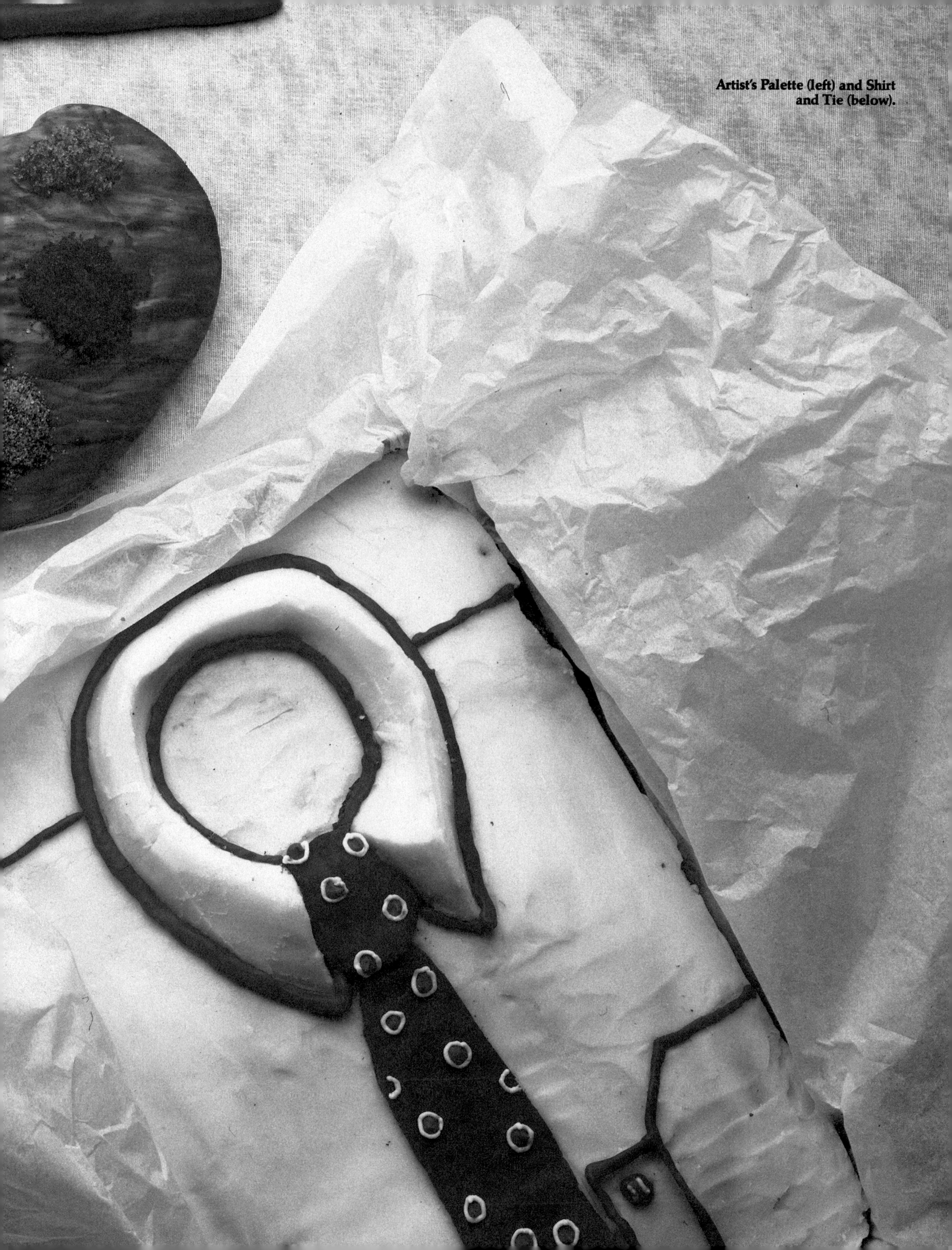

450g (16oz) marzipan
Sugar flowers
Coconut mushrooms, if available
50g (2oz) desiccated coconut
Candle and holder

Put the cakes on top of one another. Cut them in an irregular 'T' shape with a round top. Use the butter cream to sandwich the cakes together. Stand the cakes up so they resemble a 'T' shape on a 23cm (9 inch) heart-shaped cake board. Brush the sandwiched cakes with the apricot glaze. Roll out the marzipan and cover the cake with a thin layer. Divide the moulding icing into two and colour half red. Roll out the red moulding icing reserving 50g (2oz) to cover the top bar of the 'T' and use egg white to brush the marzipan so the icing will adhere. Roll out the white icing reserving 100g (4oz) and use it to cover the non-iced section of the cake. Roll out the reserved 100g (4oz) of white moulding icing and cut small circles. Dot them on the red roof. Roll out the 50g (2oz) of the red moulding icing and cut 2 circles for windows 2.5cm (1 inch) across and a rectangle for a door. Colour a little royal green and pipe leaves on the side of the house. Pipe the curtains on the windows and the arch round the door. Use the sugar flowers to decorate the house and garden. Put the desiccated coconut in a bowl with a few drops of green colouring, mix well and use the coconut to decorate the board like grass. Stand the coconut mushrooms on the grass and put the candle holder with candle on the roof to represent the chimney.

Snowman

900ml (1½ pint) pudding basin
  quick mix cake
300ml (½ pint) pudding basin quick
  mix cake; use a 1.5 litre (2 pint)
  mixture altogether
Recipe American frosting
A few round candy-coated sweets or
  liquorice sweets for buttons and
  features
20cm (8 inch) length of ribbon
Paper hat, optional

the remaining 20.2x18.8cm (8½x7 inch) cake on a cake board. Sandwich the pointed cake to the top of the large cake then sandwich the 5cm (2 inch) strip on top of that to form a cabin. Brush the two pieces of cake with apricot glaze. Colour the moulding icing with your favourite colour and roll it out to cover the ship. Using a piping bag fitted with a writing nozzle and filled with royal icing, write the name of the ship and pipe on the doors and windows. Use a little icing to secure the liquorice sweet on top of the cabin as a funnel. Cotton wool may be used to simulate smoke. Colour the butter icing with a little blue food colouring and spoon it over the large cake to form waves. Use a fork to peak the icing, but do not overmix or the icing will go green! Put the sandwich flag at the front of the boat and with a little icing, stick the mints onto the deck to represent life belts.

Radio

20cm (8 inch) round quick mix cake
Recipe apricot glaze
Recipes gelatine or moulding icing
175g (6oz) jam
Food colouring – brown, pink, black,
  non-toxic gold
1 egg white, beaten
Recipe royal icing

Cut a crescent off one side of the cake so it will stand up on its side. Place the cake on a 9-inch square cake board. Brush the cake all over with apricot glaze. Tint the icing pink and roll it out. Cover the cake completely and leave to dry. Take the remaining icing, re-mould it and tint it a little darker. Roll it out into a rectangle and cut into 6 strips to make the starburst. Cut two circles for the knobs and a semi-circle for the dial. Stick all the decoration on the cake with egg white. Fill a piping bag with royal

icing and fit it with a writing nozzle. Pipe the mesh by piping diagonally between the starburst. Pipe on the lines for the dial, tuner knob and 'on/off' switch. Finally, pipe a decorative triangle on the board under each knob, with another smaller triangle over the top. Leave the icing to dry. Using a small paintbrush, paint the mesh and trim with non-toxic gold food colouring and the inside of the mesh with diagonal lines of black food colouring.

House on the Hill

2 29x21x4cm (11½x8½x1½ inch)
  quick mix cakes
2 recipe apricot glaze
1½ recipe moulding icing
Food colourings – red, green
Recipe butter icing
Recipe royal icing

This page: Radio Cake. Facing page: House on the Hill (top) and Pugwash at Sea (bottom).

When the cakes have cooled on a wire rack, trim the smaller cake round the wider edge to round it off. Spread the jam on the top of the larger cake and sit the smaller on top of the larger cake to form the head and body on the cake board. Cover the cakes completely with the American frosting. Select the candy-coated sweets or liquorice assortment sweets for features and buttons. Decorate with a hat and a ribbon scarf.

Kitchen

20cm (8 inch) square Madeira cake
Recipe royal icing
Recipe apricot glaze
450g (1lb) moulding icing
Food colourings – red, green, orange, silver

Toffee Water
225g (8oz) granulated sugar
150ml (5 fl oz) water
Sugar thermometer, if available

Cut the cake in half and form an 'L' shape on a 30cm (12 inch) cake board. Halfway along one piece of cake, cut a 2.5cm (1 inch) square hole. Roll out half the moulding icing and brush the cake with apricot glaze and use the icing to cover the 'L' shape. Colour three-quarters of the remaining icing red and use half rolled out and laid on the inside of the rectangle of the 'L'. Using a knife, mark 1cm (½ inch) squares and press down gently. Do not cut through the icing. Roll out the remaining red icing and cut into small squares to form tiles for the work surface. Spread the rectangle of cake, without the hole cut into it, with a little royal icing and stick down the small squares with a little icing surrounding each. Cut 2x5cm (2 inch) squares and use one to line the hole, gently pushing in the corners. Place the other square alongside as a draining board. Use a knife to indent the board.

To Make Taps
Take a pinch from the remaining white icing and roll out into a small sausage shape. Cut into half and with a small pair of scissors snip lengthways down the end once and again crossing the cut. Splay out the 4 pieces. Curl the other end of the sausage to form the waterspout. Repeat with the other

small sausage shape and leave them both to dry.

To Make the Vegetables
Take a pinch from the remaining white moulding icing. Colour it green and shape about two-thirds into a small ball for the heart of the cabbage. Shape the remainder into 8 leaves and arrange the leaves around the heart, overlapping each one. Press gently so that they adhere to one another. Taking another pinch from the white, colour it orange and shape into small cones. Make a little piece green and cut out some stalks. Press them to the tops of the carrot. To make the peas, shape any small pieces of green moulding icing into balls. Colour a small pinch of moulding icing red and form into small balls. Make more green stalks and, with a cocktail stick, dent the top of each ball and push in a little green stalk to make tomatoes.

To Make Plates
Roll out any odd pieces of coloured moulding icing into tiny balls. Mould a few round the end of a pencil and flatten some gently. Reserve them until you have made the sugar water. Colour a little royal icing red and use to fill a piping bag fitted with a writing nozzle. Pipe the knobs and drawers on the inside of the kitchen. Using a small paintbrush, paint the taps with silver non-toxic colouring. Leave them to dry.

To Make the Sugar Water
Heat the sugar and water so that the sugar dissolves and boils. Continue to boil the mixture until it reaches a soft crack point – that is, just before it starts to colour. If a sugar thermometer is available, the reading should be 132-143°C or 270-290°F. Pour the sugar mixture into the sink and push in the plates and dishes before it sets. Using a little royal icing, put the taps into place.

The Mouse that got the Cheese

20cm (8 inch) square Madeira sponge
2 x recipe butter icing
2 eyes, as used in dollmaking
1 metre (1 yard) pink cord
2 x 5cm (2 inch) diameter teardrop shapes of pink paper
1 jelly sweet
2 cocktail sticks
Food colouring – black

Mouse
Cut the cake diagonally and stand it upright on the diagonal line. Round the top of the triangle to give the mouse a smooth back. With a little black food colouring, colour half the butter icing so it is light grey. Cover all the exposed areas of the cake and peak it gently with a fork. Cut 30cm (12 inches) of pink cord and attach it to one

end for a tail. Cut 4x15cm (6 inch) lengths and knot them all in the middle. Push them onto the front of his face, placing the jelly sweet on the knot. Attach the tear drop shapes to the side of his head for ears using the cocktail sticks. Place an eye on each side of his head.

Cheese
Put the remaining triangle on one end and, with a melon baller, scoop out little holes. Cover the cake with the remaining butter icing and smooth gently with a palette knife.

Christmas Pudding

This makes a quick, non-iced Christmas cake which acts as a centrepiece for a party, or for a family Christmas.

23cm (9 inch) recipe for rich fruit cake baked in a 1 litre (1½ pint) ovenproof pudding basin
90ml (6 tblsp) brandy
225g (8oz) marzipan
Recipe apricot glaze
½ recipe royal icing
Holly to decorate

After cooking, soak the fruit cake with the brandy. As the cake is not iced, this will keep it moist. Put the cake on a cake board or plate. Roll out the marzipan into a circle and push it into an irregular shape, like a little island with coves. Brush the top and a little way down the cake with the apricot glaze. Cover the top and the sides of the cake with the marzipan. Fit a piping bag with a large star nozzle and fill with royal icing. Pipe large stars round the base of the cake. Decorate with real, marzipan or artificial holly.

This page: **Kitchen (top)** and **The Mouse that got the Cheese (bottom)**.

Facing page: Snowman and Christmas Pudding Cake.

Tea Time Treats

Baking at home is not as difficult as some might expect and in very little time one can create some appetising treats for the tea table. Here are lots of recipes which may tempt you to try them for yourself at picnics, birthdays and tea parties.

Scones

PREPARATION TIME: 15 minutes

COOKING TIME: 10-15 minutes

OVEN TEMPERATURE: 200°C, 400°F, Gas Mark 6

225g (8oz) plain flour
5ml (1 tsp) cream of tartar
2.5ml (½ tsp) bicarbonate of soda
Good pinch of salt
40g (1½oz) butter or margarine
75g (3oz) caster sugar
40g (1½oz) sultanas
15g (½oz) sugared ginger pieces
15g (½oz) sunflower seeds
2 eggs, plus a little milk if required
1 egg, beaten or a little milk for glazing

Sieve the dry ingredients twice. Rub in the fat, add sugar, sultanas, ginger pieces and sunflower seeds and mix to a soft dough with eggs. Knead lightly on floured surface. Roll out to approximately 1cm (½ inch) thickness. Place on floured baking sheet and brush the top with beaten egg or milk. Bake in the oven for 10-15 minutes.

Walnut Cake

PREPARATION TIME: 15 minutes

COOKING TIME: 35 minutes

OVEN TEMPERATURE: 180°C, 350°F, Gas Mark 4

4 eggs
175g (6oz) caster sugar
125g (4oz) plain sifted flour
15ml (1 tblsp) oil
125g (4oz) walnuts, finely chopped
Recipe butter cream
Walnut halves to decorate

Grease and line two 20cm (8 inch) sandwich tins. Place the eggs and sugar in a heatproof bowl and whisk over a pan of hot, but not boiling, water until thick (see whisked sponge method). Partially fold in the flour, add the oil and chopped walnuts and fold in gently. Divide the mixture between the prepared tins and bake in the oven for 35 minutes. When the cake is cooked, it will spring back when touched. Turn onto a wire rack to cool. Split each cake in half and fill with butter cream. Swirl the remaining butter cream on top of the cake and decorate with walnut halves.

Welsh Cakes (above), Walnut Cake (right) and Scones (far right).

Welsh Cakes

PREPARATION TIME: 15 minutes
COOKING TIME: 8 minutes
(4 minutes per side)
OVEN TEMPERATURE: 140°C,
275°F, Gas Mark 1

100g (4oz) self-raising flour
Pinch of salt
40g (1½oz) butter or margarine
40g (1½oz) sugar
1 egg, plus a little milk if required
40g (1½oz) currants
2.5ml (½ tsp) ground nutmeg

Sieve the flour and salt. Rub in the
fat and stir in sugar, nutmeg and
currants. Mix to a pastry
consistency with egg. Roll out to
6mm (¼ inch) thickness and cut
with a 6mm small pastry cutter.
Cook on baking stone or large
greased pan. Switch oven off for 15
minutes then grease and reheat for
second batch. Dredge with caster
sugar and serve. Makes 10.

Flapjacks

PREPARATION TIME: 15 minutes

COOKING TIME: 30 minutes

OVEN TEMPERATURE: 180°C, 350°F, Gas Mark 4

125g (4oz) margarine
125g (4oz) soft brown sugar
75g (3oz) golden syrup
250g (8oz) rolled oats

Melt the margarine, sugar and syrup in a bowl over a pan of hot water. Stir in the rolled oats and mix thoroughly. Grease a shallow 20cm (8 inch) square tin. Turn the mixture into the tin and smooth down the top. Bake in the oven for 30 minutes until golden. Cool in the tin for 3 minutes before cutting into fingers. Remove from tin when cool. Makes 16.

Coconut Specials

PREPARATION TIME: 20 minutes

COOKING TIME: 30 minutes

OVEN TEMPERATURE: 160°C, 325°F, Gas Mark 3

225g (8oz) puff pastry
A little jam, melted
50g (2oz) melted butter
100g (4oz) desiccated coconut
100g (4oz) sugar
2 eggs

Roll out the puff pastry. Using a round pastry cutter, cut rounds and use to line a patty tin. Using a pastry brush, coat the pastry with a little jam. Beat together the butter, coconut, sugar and eggs. Divide the coconut mixture between the patty tins. Bake in the oven for 30 minutes until golden brown. When cooked, remove from tin and cool on a wire rack. Makes 14.

Victoria Sponge

PREPARATION TIME: 30 minutes

COOKING TIME: 20-25 minutes

OVEN TEMPERATURE: 190°C, 375°F, Gas Mark 5

125g (4oz) butter or margarine
125g (4oz) caster sugar
2 eggs
125g (4oz) self-raising flour, sifted
with a pinch of salt
15ml (1 tblsp) hot water

45ml (3 tblsp) jam
150ml (¼ pint) double cream,
whipped
Caster sugar

Grease and line 2x18cm (7 inch) sandwich tins. Cream the fat and sugar until light and fluffy. Beat in the eggs singly and fold in 15ml (1 tblsp) of flour with each egg. Fold in the remaining flour, then add the hot water. Divide the mixture between the tins and bake in the oven for 20-25 minutes until the cakes are golden. When the cakes are cooked, they spring back when lightly pressed. Turn the cakes onto a wire rack to cool. Sandwich the cakes together with jam and cream. Sprinkle the top with caster sugar.

Chocolate Fudge Triangles

PREPARATION TIME: 25 minutes

COOKING TIME: 30 minutes for base, 10 minutes for topping

OVEN TEMPERATURE: 180°C, 350°F, Gas Mark 4

125g (4oz) butter
50g (2oz) caster sugar
175g (6oz) plain flour

Fudge Topping
125g (4oz) butter
50g (2oz) caster sugar
30ml (2 tblsp) golden syrup
150ml (5 fl oz) condensed milk
125g (4oz) plain chocolate

Cream the butter and sugar together until fluffy. Add the flour and stir until the mixture binds. Knead until smooth. Roll out and press into a shallow 20cm (8 inch) square tin. Prick with a fork and bake in the oven for 30 minutes. Cool in the tin. Put the ingredients for the topping in a heavy saucepan and stir until dissolved. Slowly boil and stir for 7 minutes. Cool the topping a little and spread over the biscuit base. Leave it to set. When set, cut into squares, then cut diagonally to make triangles.

Lemon July Cake

PREPARATION TIME: 30 minutes

COOKING TIME: 25 minutes

OVEN TEMPERATURE: 190°C, 375°F, Gas Mark 5

Base
100g (4oz) butter or margarine
100g (4oz) sugar
1 egg, beaten
175g (6oz) self-raising flour

1st Topping
150ml (¼ pint) water
45ml (3 tblsp) sugar
15ml (1 tblsp) cornflour
Juice of two lemons

2nd Topping
150ml (¼ pint) milk
5ml (1 tsp) cornflour
25g (1oz) butter
75g (3oz) sugar
Desiccated coconut to sprinkle

Base
Cream the butter and sugar, add the egg and flour and pour into a tin and press down. Bake in the oven for 20 minutes.

1st Topping
Mix the water with the cornflour to make a paste. Boil with the other ingredients until the mixture begins to thicken, stirring constantly. Spread on the cooked cake base while the mixture is still warm.

2nd Topping
Boil milk and cornflour until it thickens. Add the the butter and sugar, creamed. Mix well and spread on top of the July. Sprinkle with the desiccated coconut, cut into fingers and serve.

This page: Chocolate Brownies (top), Chocolate Fudge Triangles (centre) and Flapjacks (bottom).

Facing page: Victoria Sponge (top right), Lemon July Cake (centre left) and Coconut Specials (bottom).

Chocolate Brownies

PREPARATION TIME: 25 minutes

COOKING TIME: 35 minutes

OVEN TEMPERATURE: 180°C, 350°F, Gas Mark 4

125g (4oz) self-raising flour
1.25ml (¼ tsp) baking powder
125g (4oz) plain chocolate
50g (2oz) butter
125g (4oz) soft brown sugar
2 eggs
75g (3oz) walnuts
75g (3oz) mixed fruit

Icing
125g (4oz) plain chocolate
15g (½oz) butter

Sift the flour and baking powder together in a bowl. Melt the chocolate in a bowl over a small saucepan of hot water. Cream the butter for the brownies with the sugar until light and fluffy. Beat in the eggs separately, adding the flour with the second egg. Beat the melted chocolate into the mixture, then fold in the walnuts and fruit. Grease and line a shallow 20cm (8 inch) square tin and bake in the oven for 35 minutes. Cut into squares while still warm and cool in the tin.

Spiced Biscuits

PREPARATION TIME: 20 minutes

COOKING TIME: 15 minutes

OVEN TEMPERATURE: 180°C, 350°F, Gas Mark 4

125g (4oz) wholewheat flour
2.5ml (½ tsp) bicarbonate of soda
5ml (1 tsp) ground cinnamon
5ml (1 tsp) mixed spice
50g (2oz) rolled oats
75g (3oz) sugar
75g (3oz) butter or margarine
5ml (1 tblsp) golden syrup
5ml (1 tblsp) milk

Put the flour, bicarbonate of soda, cinnamon, mixed spice, oats and sugar into a bowl. Melt the butter in a small saucepan with the syrup and milk. Pour the liquid into the dry ingredients and beat until smooth. Make the mixture into little balls and place them a little apart on a lightly-greased baking sheet. Flatten each one. Bake in the oven for 15 minutes until golden and cool on the baking sheet.

Macaroons

PREPARATION TIME: 20 minutes

COOKING TIME: 20 minutes

OVEN TEMERATURE: 180°C, 350°F, Gas Mark 4

250g (8oz) caster sugar
150g (5oz) ground almonds
15ml (1 tblsp) rice flour
2 egg whites
Rice paper
20 split almonds

Mix the sugar, almonds and rice flour together. In a separate bowl, beat the egg whites lightly and add the ready-mixed dry ingredients. Let the mixture stand for 5 minutes. Line a baking sheet with rice paper. Mould the mixture into little balls and place them on the lined baking sheet slightly apart. Gently flatten the macaroons and put an almond on each one. Bake in the oven for 20 minutes, then cool on baking sheet. Makes 20.

Almond Slices

PREPARATION TIME: 20 minutes

COOKING TIME: 20 minutes

OVEN TEMPERATURE: 200°C, 400°F, Gas Mark 6

Pastry Base
200g (8oz) plain flour
100g (4oz) butter
1.25ml (¼ tsp) salt
Cold water to mix

Topping
60ml (4 tblsp) jam
100g (4oz) caster sugar
100g (4oz) icing sugar
175g (6oz) ground almonds
1 egg, plus 1 egg white
A few drops almond essence
25g (1oz) flaked almonds to decorate

Chocolate Icing

175g (6oz) plain chocolate
30ml (2 tblsp) single cream

To Decorate

1 packet chocolate buttons
75g (3oz) chocolate sugar strands or
Whole nuts

Sift together the dry ingredients into a bowl and make a well in the centre. Add the sugar, syrup, eggs, oil and milk and beat until smooth. Grease and line a 23cm (9 inch) cake tin and pour in the cake mixture. Cook in the oven for 45-50 minutes; leave in the tin for a few minutes before turning out the cake onto a wire rack.

To Make the Chocolate Icing
Put the chocolate and cream into a small, heavy pan and heat gently until melted. Cool the mixture slightly and pour over the cake. Decorate with chocolate buttons, chocolate strands, or nuts.

Harvest Crunchies

PREPARATION TIME: 20 minutes	
COOKING TIME: 15 minutes	
OVEN TEMPERTURE: 190°C, 375°F, Gas Mark 5	

75g (3oz) self-raising flour
2.5ml (½ tsp) mixed spice
75g (3oz) wholewheat flour
25g (1oz) oatmeal
125g (4oz) butter or margarine
50g (2oz) soft brown sugar
25g (1oz) sultanas
30ml (2 tblsp) milk

Sift the flour and spice into a bowl. Stir in the wholewheat flour and oatmeal. Rub the fat into the mixture until it resembles a stiff dough by adding the milk. Flour a work surface and turn the dough out onto it. Lightly knead the dough and roll it out until very thin. With a 7.5cm (3 inch) fluted biscuit cutter, cut out rounds and place them on a lightly-greased baking sheet. Bake in the oven, then cool on a wire rack. Makes 20.

Facing page: Macaroons (top), Spiced Biscuits (right) and Harvest Crunchies (bottom left).

This page: Chocolate Fudge Cake (top), Viennese Fingers (left) and Almond Slices (bottom).

Sift the flour and salt into a bowl and rub in the butter until it resembles fine breadcrumbs. Add enough water to mix into a pliable dough. Roll out the dough onto a floured surface and use to line a greased or dampened shallow 25x15cm (10x6 inch) baking tin. Pinch the long edges to form a border. Cover the base with jam. In a clean bowl, mix together the sugars and almonds. Beat well and then add the whole egg, egg white and almond essence. Use the almond mixture to cover the jam, spreading evenly with a knife. Sprinkle with almonds. Bake in the oven for 20 minutes until well risen and golden. When cooked, cut in the tin and leave to cool for 10 minutes. Then remove from tin and leave to finish cooling on a wire rack.

Viennese Fingers

PREPARATION TIME: 20 minutes	
COOKING TIME: 15 minutes	
OVEN TEMPERATURE: 180°C, 350°F, Gas Mark 4	

175g (6oz) butter or margarine
50g (2oz) icing sugar
Grated rind of 1 orange
125g (4oz) plain flour
50g (2oz) cornflour

Cream together the butter, sugar and orange rind until fluffy. Sieve the flour and cornflour together and beat well into the mixture. Fill a piping bag fitted with a 2.5cm (1 inch) fluted nozzle and pipe 7.5cm (3 inch) fingers, well separated, on a sheet of non-stick silicone paper. Bake in the oven for 15 minutes

and, when cooked, transfer to a wire rack to cool. If required, two fingers can be sandwiched together with a little apricot jam. Makes 12.

Chocolate Fudge Cake

PREPARATION TIME: 15 minutes	
COOKING TIME: 45-50 minutes	
OVEN TEMPERATURE: 160°C, 325°F, Gas Mark 3	

200g (7oz) plain flour
5ml (1 tsp) bicarbonate of soda
5ml (1 tsp) baking powder
30ml (2 tblsp) cocoa powder
150g (5oz) soft brown sugar
30ml (2 tblsp) golden syrup
2 eggs
150ml (¼ pint) oil
300ml (½ pint) milk

Celebration Cakes

Pipe a row of stars round the bottom of the cake. With a medium, plain nozzle pipe bulbs between each of the stars on the inner edge of the cake. Pipe another row of bulbs on the side of the cake above the stars. Colour a little of the icing pink and fit a piping bag with a writing nozzle. Pipe a row of dropped loops from each of the bulbs on the top of the cake. From the point of alternate stars on the top edge of the cake, pipe a row of dropped loops. Go round the cake again piping loops on the stars omitted on the first round. Pipe a bulb on the point of each of the stars. With the pink icing, pipe a scallop on the cake board round the stars. Pipe the message with swirls round it in the shape of 'S's and 'C's on the top of the cake and place the flowers, a little fern and the ribbon in position.

Boy's Birthday Cake

20cm (8 inch) square, rich fruit cake
Recipe apricot glaze
800g (1¾lb) marzipan
Royal icing, made with 1.4kg (3lb)
*   icing sugar*
Food colouring – blue
8 silver leaves for the top
16 silver leaves for the side panels

Brush the top of the cake with the apricot glaze. Cover the cake with the marzipan and leave it to dry. Attach the cake to the board with a little icing. Flat ice the sides and the top of the cake and let it dry. Fit a piping bag with a large nozzle and pipe a continuous 'S' pattern on the top edge and the base of the cake. Pipe 4 bars horizontally

Mother's Day Cake

18cm (7 inch) or 20cm (8 inch)
*   square or round cake*
Recipe apricot glaze
675g (1½lb) marzipan
Royal icing, made with 900g (2lb)
*   icing sugar*
Food colourings – green, yellow
Green ribbon
Piped flowers

Brush the top and sides of the cake with apricot glaze and cover with marzipan; leave to dry. With a little icing, attach the cake to the cake board and flat ice the top and sides; leave to dry. Using a piping bag fitted with a leaf nozzle, pipe a row of leaves in white icing facing outwards around the bottom of the cake. Then pipe an overlapping circle of white leaves around the top edge of the cake. Fill another piping bag with green-coloured icing and pipe a row of leaves facing outwards on top. Finally, pipe an overlapping circle of green leaves on the top. Fill a piping bag with a little yellow-coloured icing and fit a medium writing nozzle and write 'Mother' on the top surface of the cake. Attach the piped flowers on the top surface with a dab of icing and, using the piping bag with green icing and the leaf nozzle again, pipe a few leaves around the flowers to finish. Decorate with the green ribbon.

Girl's Birthday Cake

20cm (8 inch) round, rich fruit cake
Recipe apricot glaze
800g (1¾lb) marzipan
Royal icing, made with 1.4kg (3lb)
*   icing sugar*
3 piped flowers
Food colouring – pink
Pink ribbon
Frond of asparagus fern

Brush the top and the sides of the cake with apricot glaze. Cover the cake with the marzipan. Attach the cake to the board with a little icing. Flat ice the top and the sides of the cake. Fit a piping bag with a large star nozzle and pipe a circle of stars round the top edge of the cake.

This page: Girl's Birthday Cake and Boy's Birthday Cake.

Facing page: Mother's Day Cake.

across and down the corners of the cake. At each of the 4 corners, and on the top of the cake, pipe a single line from the flat surface of the cake crossing the continuous 'S' and ending in the corner. Fit a small star nozzle and pipe vertically down the corners of the cake, covering the ends of the bars. Pipe the decorative lines on the top of the cake, starting with a long line with a dot at each end and working out and down with shorter lines towards the outer edge. Write the name in the centre of the cake. Colour a little of the icing blue and fit a writing nozzle onto the piping bag. Pipe 2 rows of scallops on the top edge of the cake, a row on each side of the continuous 'S', ending at the corner where the corner bars start. Overpipe the name in blue. Pipe a dropped loop round the base of the cake, with the point of the loops at each of the corners. Attach 2 silver leaves at the base corners of each of the 4 side panels, and 2 silver leaves on the top of the cake at each of the 4 corners, attached to the flat surface of the cake.

Silver Wedding Anniversary Cake

20 or 23cm (8 or 9 inch) square, rich
  fruit cake
Recipe apricot glaze
800-900g (1¾-2lb) marzipan
Royal icing, made with 1.25kg
  (2½lb) icing sugar
8 silver leaves
Silver non-toxic colouring

Brush the top and the sides of the cake with apricot glaze and cover with marzipan. Leave the cake to dry. Attach the cake to the board with a little icing. Flat ice the top and sides of the cake, giving 2 or 3 coats. Fit your piping bag with a medium writing nozzle. Using a saucepan lid or a round template, draw a circle in the centre of the top of the cake. Using a medium-sized five-star nozzle, pipe a continuous swirl round the bottom edge of the cake and finish off each corner with a shell. With a smaller star nozzle, pipe a small dot on the top edge of the cake in the centre of the top edge of each of the side panels and divide the space

It is most important that a celebration cake should feed the desired number of guests, so here is a guide:

Round	Square	Portions
15cm (6 inch)	13cm (5 inch)	20-30
20cm (7½-8 inch)	18cm (7 inch)	40-45
25cm (10 inch)	23cm (9 inch)	70-80
28cm (11 inch)	25cm (10 inch)	100-110
30cm (12 inch)	30cm (12 inch)	130-140

NB: for decorating simple cakes, sweets can be utilised and are easily applied to butter icing. These are much used in novelty cake designs.

between the original dot and the corner of the cake with a further dot. You should have 3 dots on each of the top sides of the cake. Using these as a guide, join them together by piping a scallop, with the dots marking the points of the scallop. Using a writing nozzle, pipe with a scribbling line between the scallop on the sides of the cake and the template circle drawn on the top of the cake. The scribbling should be done with a continuous line that never crosses itself. Using the same nozzle, overpipe the template-drawn circle with a continuously twisting line. On the side panels and on the corners of

the cake, pipe three beads in descending size below each of the points of the scallop. Overpipe the continuous swirls round the bottom of the cake with a plain, continuous swirl beginning and ending with an 'S' shape. Pipe the '25' in the circle on top of the cake, then – when dry – overpipe this again with white. Fit your piping bag with a medium star nozzle and, having positioned the silver leaves, secure them with a piped rosette. Using a fine paintbrush, gently paint the continuous swirl overpiped on the circle on the top surface of the cake and also the top of the '25' with a single silver line.

Silver Wedding Anniversary Cake.

Golden Wedding Cake

25cm (10 inch) round, rich fruit cake
Recipe apricot glaze
1kg (2¼lb) marzipan
Royal icing, made from 1.4kg (3lb)
 icing sugar
Food colouring – yellow
6 gold leaves
Yellow ribbon

Brush the sides and top of the cake with the apricot glaze. Cover the cake with the marzipan and leave to dry. Attach the cake to the board with a little icing. Flat ice the top and sides of the cake. Fit a piping bag with a large star nozzle and pipe a row of shells round the top of the cake. Pipe a row of shells round the bottom of the cake. Fit the piping bag with a smaller star nozzle and pipe continuous 'C's on the shells on the top of the cake. Fit the piping bag with a medium-sized plain nozzle and pipe a scallop on the top of the cake round the shells. Round the bottom of the cake, on the board, pipe a scallop round the shells. Repeat the scallop on the side of the cake under the shells on the top edge of the cake. Colour a little of the icing yellow and, using a writing nozzle, repeat the pattern of continuous 'C's on the top edge of the cake. Pipe a dropped loop on top of the shell at the base of the cake. Fit the same piping bag with a leaf nozzle and pipe inverted leaves between the shells at the base of the cake, with the point of the leaves creeping up the sides of the cake. With a writing nozzle, pipe the words and surround them with 'S's and 'C's. Decorate with a real rose or any other flower, or piped flowers and/ or gold leaves.

Diana Wedding Cake

Two-Tier Round Cake
25cm (10 inch) round, rich fruit cake
15 or 18cm (6 or 7 inch) round, rich
 fruit cake
2 x recipe apricot glaze
1.4kg (3lb) marzipan
Royal icing, made from 1.6kg (3½lb)
 icing sugar
Silver cake boards: 33cm (13 inch)
 and 20 or 23cm (8 or 9 inch)
32 silver leaves
8 piped flowers
4 round pillars

Brush the top and sides of the cake with apricot glaze and cover with

marzipan. Leave the cake to dry. Attach the cake to the board with a little icing. Flat ice the top and sides of the cake, giving three coats and an extra coat on the base cake. Fit a piping bag with a large star nozzle and pipe shells round the bottom of each of the cakes. Using the same nozzle, mark the cake surface lightly at the edge as though it were square. That is, treat it as though it had four corners, putting a dab of icing in each of the four corners and a smaller dab at the centre of each of the four sides. From each of the

dabs which mark the centre of the sides pipe an inverted 'S', finishing at the corner mark. Repeat this from where you started and mirror the original shape towards the other corner point. Repeat this round the cake. Pipe a 'C' facing the centre of the cake, with its back marking the centre point of the side. Overpipe all the decorative swirls, the 'S's and 'C's twice. Fit a piping bag with a medium-sized plain nozzle and pipe a continuously twisting scallop on the upper edge of the sides of the cakes. Repeat this pattern on the

cake board around the shells. With the same nozzle overpipe the decorative swirls, 'S's and 'C's on the tops of the cakes. Pipe a scallop on the top surface of the cake, encompassing the 'C's in the curves; three curves to each

This page: Golden Wedding Cake. Facing page: Diana Wedding Cake.

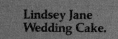

Lindsey Jane Wedding Cake.

imaginary side. Pipe dropped loops under the continuously twisting scallop on the sides of cakes. On the sides of the cake below the loops, attach the flowers and leaves with a little icing, four flowers per cake below each 'C' and an icing rosette to attach the other leaves between each of the flowers. Assemble the cake using the pillars and decorate the top with flowers.

Lindsey Jane Wedding Cake

Two-Tier Square Cake
15cm (6 inch) square, rich fruit cake
25cm (10 inch) square, rich fruit cake
2 x recipe apricot glaze
1.5kg (3¼lb) marzipan
Royal icing made with 1.75kg (4lb) icing sugar
28 pink piped roses, to decorate
Asparagus fern, to decorate
Silver cake boards, 20cm (8 inch) and 30cm (12 inch)
4 square pillars
2 narrow ribbon bows

This design is suitable for a 1, 2 or 3-tier cake. The roses are chosen to match the bridal attire.
Brush the sides and tops of the cakes with apricot glaze and cover with marzipan. Leave to dry. Attach the cakes to the cake boards with a dab of icing. Flat ice the cakes, giving two or three coats all over. Fit a piping bag with a medium-sized shell nozzle and pipe shells on the top edge, the bottom edge and up each of the corners of the cakes. Pipe on the top of the cakes in each corner 2 shells facing each other. Fit the piping bag with a medium-sized plain nozzle and pipe a shallow scallop round the top side of the cake. Pipe with an 'S'-shaped swirl, filling each of the small scallops. On the bottom tier, put a cluster of roses in the middle of the cake, surrounded by fern, two roses in each of the corners and one rose at the base of each of the corners. On the top tier, repeat but with a single rose at the top of each corner and the ribbon bows on top of the cake. Assemble the cake using the pillars.

Christening Cake

20cm (8 inch) round, rich fruit cake
Recipe apricot glaze
800g (1¾lb) marzipan
Royal icing, made with 1.4kg (3lb) icing sugar
Food colouring – blue
15g (½oz) marzipan
1 narrow, white ribbon bow

Brush the top and sides of the cake with the apricot glaze. Cover the cake with the marzipan and leave it to dry. Attach the cake to the board with the royal icing. Fit a piping bag with a large star nozzle. With an icing comb, comb the sides of the cake with a swirling line and pipe a row of shells round the top of the cake. Fit a piping bag with a small star nozzle and pipe a scallop round the top of the shells. Pipe a graduated rope round the bottom of the cake, with a large, dropped loop round the rope. Fit the piping bag with a small, plain nozzle and pipe a scallop on the top of the cake next to the shells. Pipe the name of the baby on the top of the cake. Colour a little royal icing blue. Using a writing nozzle, pipe beads at the points of each of the nozzles. Pipe another scallop onto the silver board. Pipe over the name with the blue, piping small 'C's and scrolls. To make the bootees, colour a little moulding icing pale blue and shape into two. Press a small hole towards the end of each of the oval shapes. With a writing nozzle, pipe round the holes, making a little bow at the front. Decorate with a silver ball and put the small bow between the bootees.

Tracy Rose Wedding Cake

Three-Tier Square
13cm (5 inch) square, rich fruit cake
20cm (8 inch) square, rich fruit cake
28cm (11 inch) square, rich fruit cake
3 x recipe apricot glaze
2.25kg (5lb) marzipan
Royal icing, made with 3.3kg (8lb) icing sugar
2 x recipe moulding icing, peach colour (to make 60 moulded roses)
3 cake boards: 18cm (7 inch), 25cm (10 inch) and 35cm (14 inch)
Food colourings – green, peach (brown)
8 square cake pillars
2 rectangular silver boards

Brush the top and sides of the cakes with apricot glaze and cover with marzipan; leave to dry. Attach the cakes to the silver cake boards with a dab of icing. Flat ice the tops of the cakes with the royal icing, which is tinted peach in colour. Cut the thin, rectangular cake boards lengthways down the middle and then cut each widthways with a sharp knife. Cut the corners off each piece diagonally so that they will go together to form a square with a square hole in the centre. Place each on a sheet of greaseproof paper and flat ice onto the white side with a palette knife; leave to dry. Fill a piping bag with a medium writing nozzle and the other with a basket weave nozzle. Hold the basket weave nozzle sideways and on the side of the first cake pipe 3 lines, evenly spaced, one above the other and all of the same length. Pipe a vertical line using the writing nozzle along the edge of the basket weaving. Continue this process until the cake is covered. Repeat the basket weave method on each of the cardboard lids. To make the moulded flowers see chapter on decorations. Colour a little of the royal icing green and fit a piping bag with a leaf nozzle. Colour a little more royal icing a dark peach and use it to fill a bag fitted with a star nozzle. Continue to use the writing nozzle filled with the tinted peach royal icing as used in the basket weave. Position the moulded icing roses facing outward round the top edges of the 2 bottom tiers and in a radiating pattern on the small top tier. Pipe dark peach stars between each of the roses and dot the centre of each star using the tinted

peach royal icing. Pipe leaves at random round the flowers. Place the pillars on a tray and pipe small stars dotted with tinted peach for the centre of the flower. Again, pipe leaves at random and leave to dry.

To Assemble the Cake
Place the basket lids round the outer edge of each of the cake's bottom two tiers and, with a little icing, secure them to the top of the cake. Make sure that there is enough room in the square at the centre of each cake for the four pillars.
Note: the cake board can be iced with a palette knife to surround each of the cakes, if required.

This page: Christening Cake.

Facing page: Tracy Rose Wedding Cake.

nozzle, pipe the words 'God Bless' and, with inverted 'S's and 'C's, pipe little swirls around the words. Pipe the starbursts round the cross. Decorate with the ribbon.

Fiona Anne Wedding Cake

Three-Tier Round
15cm (6 inch) round, rich fruit cake
20cm (8 inch) round, rich fruit cake
25cm (10 inch) round, rich fruit cake
3 x recipe apricot glaze
1.75kg (4lb) marzipan
Royal icing, made with 3kg (7lb) icing sugar
60 silver leaves
30 piped sugar roses, painted with non-toxic silver food colouring
Silver cake boards: 20cm (8 inch), 25cm (10 inch) and 33cm (13 inch)
8 round cake pillars

Brush the top and the sides of the cake with apricot glaze, cover with marzipan and leave to dry. Attach the cakes to the cake boards with a dab of icing. Flat ice the cakes, giving three coats all over and an extra coat for the tops. Fit a piping bag with a large star nozzle and pipe inverted shells with the tail of the shell going up the side of the cake. With the same nozzle, pipe 'C's round the top edge of each of the cakes and leave to dry. Pipe a further 'C' on top of the first. Fit the piping bag with a medium plain nozzle and pipe a further 'C' on top of the original two. Working along the side edge of the cakes, pipe a dropped loop with a swirling action to create a graduated rope. With a plain writing nozzle, pipe a dropped loop round the tail of each of the base shells, missing out a shell as you pipe. When you have gone round the cake, repeat the process, crossing the dropped loop from the tail of the shell that you missed out on the first round. On the tops of the cakes, pipe a scallop round each of the 'C' shapes. Fit the

Confirmation Cake

20 or 23cm (8 or 9 inch) square, rich fruit cake
Recipe apricot glaze
800-900g (1¾-2lb) marzipan
Royal icing, made with 1.25kg (2½lb) icing sugar
Food colouring – violet
Violet ribbon

Brush the top and the sides of the cake with apricot glaze and cover with marzipan. Leave the cake to dry. Attach the cake to the board with a little icing. Flat ice the top and the sides of the cake, giving 2 or 3 coats. Fit a piping bag with a medium-sized 5-point nozzle and pipe a row of graduated ropes round the top edge of the cake. To do this, start from the centre of one side and mark with a small dot of icing. Divide the area between the corners of the cake and the original dot with another dot and work your way round each of the sides of the cake. You now have 3 dots on each side of the cake. Pipe between each of the dots in a continuous swirl which gets thicker at the halfway mark and decreases in size towards the end. Repeat the graduated ropes round the bottom edge of the cake. Fit the piping bag with a smaller star nozzle and pipe a scallop round each of the graduated ropes. You should have 4 on each side of the cake on both the top edge and the bottom. On the flat surface of the cake, pipe a scallop using the same nozzle as before, but facing outwards, so you have concave and convex scallops on the top edge of the cake. Fit the piping bag with a plain writing nozzle and overpipe the first scallop with a continuously twisting line. Fit another piping bag with a little violet-coloured icing and, towards one side of the top of the cake, pipe the outer line of the cross with a continuous line. Take a little white icing and thin it with a small amount of lemon juice until it flows. When the violet-coloured outline of the cross is dry, flood the shape with the liquid icing. Burst any bubbles and leave it to dry. With the violet icing and writing

This page: Confirmation Cake.

Facing page: Fiona Anne Wedding Cake.

piping bag with the medium plain nozzle and pipe a bead to conceal the tail of each of the base shells.

To Decorate
Reserve 15 roses for the bottom cake, 10 for the middle tier and 5 for the top tier. Reserve 30 silver leaves for the bottom cake, 20 for the middle tier and 10 for the top tier. Space the decorations as follows: 1 rose, with twinned silver leaves on either side, with a piped forget-me-not (using a forget-me-not nozzle) to secure the leaves and a single rose placed slightly lower down on the side of the cake, followed by another rose and surrounded by twin silver leaves. Assemble the cake using the pillars and decorate the top with flowers.

Valentine Cake

20 or 23cm (8 or 9 inch) round, rich
   fruit cake, cut to a heart shape
Recipe apricot glaze
675g (1½lb) marzipan
Royal icing, made with 1.4kg (3lb)
   icing sugar
Red and cream moulded roses
Food colouring – green
Red ribbon

Brush the top and sides of the cake with apricot glaze and cover with marzipan; leave to dry. With a little icing, attach the cake to the cake board and flat ice the top and sides; leave to dry. Pipe two rows of shells around the base of the cake in white icing. Attach the red and cream moulded roses with a dab of icing on the top surface of the cake. Colour a little icing with the green food colouring and, using a leaf nozzle, pipe a few leaves round the moulded roses. Make a bow with the red ribbon and attach to the top surface of the cake to finish.

Good Luck Cake

20cm (8 inch) round, rich fruit cake
Recipe apricot glaze
800g (1¾lb) marzipan
Royal icing, made with 1kg (2lb)
   sugar
Food colourings – violet, pink
25g (1oz) black moulding icing
2 silver leaves
1 silver horseshoe, small
1 narrow, black bow

Brush the top and the sides of the cake with the apricot glaze. Cover the cake with the marzipan and let

it dry. Flat ice the top and sides of the cake, having first attached the cake to the board with a little icing. With a small star nozzle, pipe a row of shells round the top edge of the cake. Pipe a row of graduated ropes round the top edge of the side of the cake. Using the same nozzle, pipe a double row of shells round the bottom of the cake. Colour a little icing pink and, with a writing nozzle, pipe a loose scallop round the inside edge of the cake on the top surface. Pipe dropped loops over the 2 rows of shells at the bottom of the cake. Colour a little icing violet and, with a writing nozzle, pipe a scallop pattern round the outer edge of the top of the cake. Repeat the pattern on the board round the cake. Pipe a small bulb on the side of the cake on the point of the pink dropped loops. Pipe the words 'Good Luck' or 'Best Wishes' on the top of the cake using a writing nozzle and violet-coloured icing. With the pink icing, pipe a line under the words and pipe a bulb at the point of the violet dropped loops. Roll out the black moulding icing and either cut out the shape of a cat, using a sharp knife, or draw the cat onto a piece of greaseproof paper and use it as a guide. When the cat has been cut out, let it dry and put it in place with a little icing. Arrange the leaves and the ribbon.

21st Birthday Cake

This design can also be used for a golden wedding or silver wedding anniversary cake. Just omit the '21' and change the colour used: either yellow balls for a golden wedding or silver balls for a silver wedding, writing your message on the top of the cake.

20 or 23cm (8 or 9 inch) square, rich
   fruit cake
Recipe apricot glaze
800-900g (1¾-2lb) marzipan
Royal icing, made with 1.25kg (2½lb)
   icing sugar
Food colouring – violet
4 medium-sized silver horseshoes

Brush the sides and top of the cake with apricot glaze. Cover the cake with the marzipan and leave to dry. Attach the cake to the board with a little icing. Flat ice the top and the sides of the cake. When the icing is dry, make a template. Alternatively, draw a circle round a small saucepan lid or fluted jelly mould, onto a piece of greaseproof

paper. Use either of these templates to mark out the top of the cake. Fit a piping bag with a large star nozzle and pipe shells round the base of the cake. Using a plain writing nozzle filled with white icing, mark a point 2.5cm (1 inch) from the top edge of the cake on each of the side panels. Make a further point halfway between the first mark and the corner of the cake. You will now have 3 dots on each of the side panels. Use them as a guide to enable you to pipe inverted scallops. The dots mark the points of each scallop and also the corner of the cake. Using your template and the same nozzle, pipe the decorative shape on the top surface of the cake. Fit your piping bag with a forget-me-not nozzle. Pipe random forget-me-nots between the scallop on the side of the cake and the template-drawn pattern on the top. Fit the piping bag with a medium, plain writing nozzle and pipe an inner circle on the flat surface of the cake echoing the shape drawn with the use of the template. Write the figures '21' and the name, if required. Colour a little of the icing violet and, using a medium nozzle, dot the centre of each flower. Pipe the violet icing in a scallop shape on the cake board, curving round each of the shells. Using a small writing nozzle, pipe over the original template-drawn line with a continuously twisting line. Overpipe the '21' and the name with the violet icing. This can be done with half straight and half continuous twists. Using a little white icing, attach the horseshoes in the centre of each of the side panels of the cake.

Flower Birthday Cake

18cm (7 inch) or 20cm (8 inch)
   round, rich fruit cake or Madeira
   cake
Recipe apricot glaze
675g (1½lb) marzipan
Recipe pink moulding icing
Selection of moulded flowers
Ribbon – colour of your choice

Brush the top and sides of the cake with apricot glaze and cover with marzipan; leave to dry. With a little icing, attach the cake to the cake board and cover with the pink moulding icing; leave to dry. Attach the moulded flowers with a dab of icing. Decorate with the ribbon.

Flower Birthday Cake and
Good Luck Cake.

Engagement Cake

20 or 23cm (8 or 9 inch) square, rich
*   fruit cake*
Recipe apricot glaze
800-900g (1¾-2lb) marzipan
Royal icing, made with 1.25kg
*   (2½lb) icing sugar*
Three piped flowers
Food colourings – pink, blue
Pink ribbon

Brush the cake with the apricot
glaze. Cover the cake with the
marzipan and let it dry. Attach the
cake to the board with a little icing.
Flat ice the top and the sides of the
cake. Fit a piping bag with a
medium star nozzle and pipe shells
round the base of the cake. Using
the same nozzle, pipe 'C's at the
corners of the cake on the top
surface of the cake. Pipe another
'C' on top of the first. On the edge
of the top of the cake, pipe a
continuous 'S' pattern and repeat it
on the top of the first row. With
the same nozzle, pipe a line on the
flat surface of the cake. Using a
writing nozzle, pipe another line on
the inside of the first line. Colour
some of the icing blue and, with a
writing nozzle, pipe another line
round the top edge of the cake.
Pipe over the 'C's in the corners of
the cake and pipe dropped loops
over the shells at the bottom of the
cake. Fit another piping bag with a
medium-sized plain nozzle. Colour
a little icing pink and use it to pipe
continuous loops, starting and
ending with an 'S'. Pipe the
message on the top of the cake and
pipe bulbs between each of the
shells where each of the blue loops
point. With the blue icing, pipe –
using a writing nozzle – small,
decorative, inverted 'C' and 'S'
shapes round the message. Attach
the piped flowers and the ribbon.

This page: 21st Birthday Cake.

**Facing page: Valentine Cake
and Engagement Cake.**

Easter and Christmas Cakes

Special cakes are traditionally used for the celebration of religious festivals; the most popular being the traditional Christmas cake and the simnel cake at Easter. Not everybody enjoys rich cake, so there are sponge variations in this book for both Easter and Christmas.

Simnel Cake

PREPARATION TIME: 40 minutes

COOKING TIME: 3 hours

OVEN TEMPERATURE: 160°C, 325°F, Gas Mark 3 reduced to 150°C, 300°F, Gas Mark 2

*20cm (8 inch) round, rich fruit cake
  mixture*
800g (1¾lb) marzipan
30ml (2 tblsp) apricot glaze
1 egg white, beaten
Ribbon to decorate

Place half the mixture in a prepared, deep cake tin. Roll out a quarter of the marzipan into a 20cm (8 inch) circle and lay it on top of the mixture. Spread the remaining mixture on the top of the marzipan. Bake in the oven for 1 hour, lower the temperature and bake for a further 2½ hours. Leave in the tin for 5 minutes and turn onto a wire rack to cool. Roll out a third of the remaining marzipan into a 20cm (8 inch) circle. Brush the top of the cake with apricot glaze. Press the marzipan circle on top of the cake and brush with beaten egg white. Shape the remaining marzipan into balls and place round the edge. Brown under a hot grill and allow to cool. Decorate with ribbon.

Daffodil Cake

23cm (9 inch) round Madeira cake
Recipe vanilla-flavoured butter icing
Moulding icing daffodil
45ml (3 tblsp) apricot jam
15ml (1 tblsp) cocoa powder

Slice the cake and spread with the jam. Use half of the butter icing and sandwich the cake together.

Spread the top of the cake with a ¼ of the remaining butter icing. Smooth it with a palette knife. Fill a piping bag with the remaining butter icing and fit it with a 5-point star nozzle. Pipe shells round the edge of the cake. Put the daffodil on the cake. Mix a little butter icing with cocoa powder. With a piping bag fitted with a writing nozzle, pipe 'Easter' on the cake, below the daffodil.

Easter Nest

*20cm (8 inch) round lemon sponge
  (whisked or Victoria)*
*1 box orange-flavoured chocolate
  sticks*
*100g (4oz) candy-coated chocolate
  speckled eggs*
Recipe lemon-flavoured butter icing

Put the cake on a plate or cake board. Cover the cake with lemon-

This page: Daffodil Cake (top) and Simnel Cake (bottom).

Facing page: Easter Cake with Chicks (top) and Easter Nest (bottom).

flavoured butter icing. Put a ribbon round the side of the cake and make a bow. Lay the orange-flavoured chocolate sticks at angles round the sides of the cake, leaving an uncovered area in the centre of the cake. Fill the centre with eggs.

Fruit Easter Cake with Chicks

PREPARATION TIME: 45 minutes	
COOKING TIME: 1 hour 30 minutes to 1 hour 45 minutes	
OVEN TEMPERATURE: 160°C, 325°F, Gas Mark 3	

175g (6oz) butter
175g (6oz) caster sugar
3 eggs
125g (4oz) plain flour
175g (6oz) mixed dried fruit
150g (5oz) self-raising flour
50g (2oz) chopped mixed peel
50g (2oz) glacé cherries, halved
Grated rind of 1 orange
75ml (5 tblsp) orange juice
1 crushed sugar cube

To Decorate
Fluffy chicks
Yellow ribbon

Cream the butter and sugar together until light and fluffy. Beat in the eggs singly, adding a little flour after each. Toss the fruit in the remaining flour with the orange rind and juice. Grease and line a 18cm (7 inch) cake tin. Fill with the mixture and smooth with the back of a spoon. Sprinkle with some of the crushed sugar cube. Bake in the oven for 1½- 1¾ hours. Turn out and cool on a wire rack. Decorate with yellow ribbon, chicks and fresh or artificial flowers. Sprinkle top of cake with remaining sugar cube.

Festive Garland

If you prefer you can make edible decorations for this cake.

20cm (8 inch) quick mix cake, baked in a ring mould
Recipe apricot glaze
Recipe butter icing
1 round cake board
Holly leaves, berries, Christmas roses, mistletoe, candle and ribbon (colour of your choice)

Split the cake and sandwich together with the glaze. Put the cake on the plate or cake board and

cover with the icing, peaking it as you go around. Press the roses, holly leaves, berries and mistletoe into the cake, leaving a gap for the bow. When the icing is dry and hard, place a candle in the centre of the ring and attach the bow in the space reserved.

Christmas Bells

18cm (7 inch) or 20cm (8 inch) square Christmas cake
Royal icing, made with 1.25kg (2½lb) sugar
½ recipe white moulding icing
100g (4oz) granulated sugar
4 sprigs of holly, real or artificial
1 metre (1 yard) narrow, white satin ribbon
Food colouring – pink

Put the cake on a silver cake board. Royal ice the cake and leave to dry between coats. Roll out the moulding icing and, using a bell shape cutter, cut 10 bells and leave them to dry on non-stick silicone paper. Mix the granulated sugar and pink food colour well until the sugar becomes pink. Sprinkle over the bells and leave to dry. Fill a piping bag, fitted with a medium-sized star nozzle, with the royal icing. Pipe a row of shells round the bottom of the cake. Pipe a border of shells round the top of the cake and a line of shells up each of the 4 corners of the cake and allow the icing to dry. Make 5 bows with the narrow, white ribbon. With a little icing sugar secure two icing bells on each side panel of the cake. The tops of the bells should be nearest to each of the 4 corners. Two of the bells should be placed in the centre of the top of the cake, with the tops of the bells together. Put a ribbon bow above each of the bells. Position the sprigs of holly in each of the four corners on top of the cake.

Christmas Tree

20cm (8 inch) square quick mix cake or rich fruit cake mix
Recipe apricot glaze
Recipe marzipan, if using fruit cake
Recipe butter icing, if using quick mix cake
450g (1lb) moulding icing

To Decorate
1 cake board
Silver balls
Desiccated coconut to sprinkle
Recipe royal icing

225g (8oz) moulding icing, white
Chocolate sticks
Gold or silver non-toxic food colouring
Food colouring – red, blue, green, yellow

Cut the cake diagonally and place the outer edges of the square next to one another, i.e. back-to-back to produce a triangular shape. If using a fruit cake, brush with apricot glaze and cover with marzipan. If using a butter icing on a quick cake mixture, cover the cake with the butter icing and leave on the cake board. Roll out the moulding icing and, using a fluted pastry cutter, cut circles and then cut each one in half and use to stick onto the butter icing. Start at the bottom edge of the cake and overlap slightly until you reach the top. With the remaining icing, make some small presents and a square tub for the tree. Cover the tree trunk with a little of the remaining butter icing and lay the cocolate sticks vertically on the tree trunk. Use any remaining icing to frost the leaves of the tree, or pipe if desired. Decorate with the silver balls and sprinkle with desiccated coconut. With the white icing to decorate, colour small pinches in various colours and, with the white royal icing, pipe strings around the various coloured shapes to make more little parcels. Roll out the remaining white icing and cut it into a star. Colour with a little non-toxic gold or silver food colouring.

Traditional Christmas Cake with Holly and Roses

18cm (7 inch) round Christmas cake
Recipe apricot glaze
675g (1½lb) marzipan
Royal icing, made with 900g (2lb) icing sugar

To Decorate
Silver balls
Christmas roses
Marzipan holly leaves and berries, small snowman or Santa, if available
Ribbon

Brush the cake with apricot glaze. Cover with the marzipan and leave to dry. Flat ice the top and sides of the cake with royal icing and leave to dry again. Use a piping bag fitted with a 5-star nozzle to pipe shells around the top edge of the cake

and then on the top, round the sides of the cake and, finally, around the bottom edge of the cake. When dry, pipe a further row between the top 2 rows using the 5-star nozzle upright to pipe stars. Decorate the top of the cake with marzipan holly and piped or moulded Christmas roses and a small snowman or Father Christmas, if desired. Tie the ribbon round the cake and make a bow. Push a silver ball into the centre of each of the stars.

Christmas Tree (right) and Festive Garland (below).

Frosted Mistletoe Cake

This is a quick and easy Christmas cake, which can be made either round or square. Any bought decorations can be used to complement the design.

18cm (7 inch) or 20cm (8 inch)
  square or round Christmas cake
Recipe apricot glaze
675g (1½lb) marzipan
900g (2lb) green moulding icing
12 mistletoe leaves and berries made
  from marzipan
60cm (2ft) x 5cm (2 inch) length of
  green ribbon
Food colouring – green

Put the cake on a silver cake board. To decorate, roll out the green moulding icing. With a small, sharp knife cut out several mistletoe leaves. Make them long and narrow with rounded ends and mark them with a knife to indicate the veins. With the uncoloured moulding icing roll small, pea-sized balls of icing to represent the berries. Use the mistletoe to decorate the top of the cake. With the ribbon, tie a large bow and attach it to the top of the cake with a little royal icing. Fill a shaker with a little icing sugar, or put it through a small sieve and shake it gently round the edge of the cake, dusting some of the mistletoe.

Christmas Candles

2 jam-filled Swiss rolls
450g (1lb) green moulding icing
100g (4oz) white moulding icing
Recipe apricot glaze
Rectangular silver cake board
Food colourings – red, yellow, blue
Red ribbon
3 cocktail sticks

Cut one Swiss roll ¾ of the way down. Brush the Swiss rolls with apricot glaze. Roll out the green moulding icing and cover the Swiss rolls. Stand them upright with something for support. In a small, heavy saucepan stir to dissolve half to three-quarters of the white

This page: Christmas Bells Cake (top) and Traditional Christmas Cake with Holly and Roses (bottom).

Facing page: Frosted Mistletoe Cake.

moulding icing. Roll out the remaining white icing on a surface dusted with icing sugar or cornflour and cut out 3 flame shapes. Leave on non-stick silicone paper to dry. When dry, paint a blue dot near the bottom; surround by yellow and edge with red. Reserve to dry. Pour the liquid moulding icing over the candles in a drizzle so that it dries like wax. Stick a flame into the top of each candle, using a cocktail stick to support them. Decorate with ribbons.

Postbox

This makes a quick and easy festive cake for those who do not like traditional Christmas cake.

1 chocolate Swiss roll
225g (8oz) red moulding icing
Recipe royal icing
Recipe apricot glaze

Roll out the moulding icing and cut out two circles to cover the ends of the Swiss roll. Roll out the remaining icing to cover the rest of the Swiss roll. Brush the Swiss roll with the apricot glaze and cover with moulding icing. Fit a piping bag with a writing nozzle and fill with some royal icing. Pipe the detail onto the postbox and leave to dry. With the remaining icing, spoon half on top of the postbox and the remainder at the bottom. Dust with a little icing sugar.

Icicles with Holly

18cm (7 inch) or 20cm (8 inch) square or round, rich fruit cake
Recipe apricot glaze
675g (1½lb) marzipan
Royal icing, made with 900g (2lb) icing sugar
Blue ribbon
Marzipan holly leaves and berries

Brush the top and sides of the cake with apricot glaze and cover with marzipan; leave to dry. With a little icing, attach the cake to the cake board and flat ice the top and sides. Leave it to dry between and after coats. Using a piping bag fitted with a shell nozzle, pipe a circle of shells on the top edge of the cake and again round the bottom of the cake. Fit the piping bag with a plain or fine-band nozzle. Place the ribbon round the sides of the cake. Pipe the icicles down and over the ribbon, varying them in length and width. Fit the piping bag with a writing nozzle and overpipe to make smaller icicles, which should hang free of the cake. Use the remaining icing to secure the holly in a pattern on top of the cake.

This page: Postbox and Christmas Candles. Facing page: Icicles with Holly.

Gâteaux

Minted Lime Gâteau

PREPARATION TIME: 35 minutes

COOKING TIME: 20 minutes

OVEN TEMPERATURE: 190°C, 375°F, Gas Mark 5

125g (4oz) caster sugar
3 eggs
75g (3oz) plain flour
40g (1½oz) melted butter
Grated rind of 1 lime
Flesh of 1 lime, de-pipped

Decoration
300ml (½ pint) double cream
1 fresh lime
Grated chocolate (optional)

Whisk the sugar and eggs together in a basin, over a saucepan of hot water, until the mixture is thick. Sieve the flour twice and fold into the whisked mixture. Mix in the lime flesh and grated rind. Grease and flour a 20cm (8 inch) cake tin and fill with the mixture. Bake in the oven for 20 minutes. Cool on a wire rack.

To Decorate
Whip the cream and spread over the gâteau, reserving a little for piping. Fill a nylon piping bag with the remaining cream and, using a star nozzle, pipe rosettes to decorate the gâteau. Sprinkle the sides with chocolate, if desired, and decorate with slices of lime.

Gâteau St Honoré

PREPARATION TIME: 1 hour 30 minutes

COOKING TIME: 30 minutes

OVEN TEMPERATURE: 160°C, 325°F, Gas Mark 3

This is a fantasy choux pastry dessert. Also known as a croquembouche, it can be built directly onto a serving stand or onto a meringue or shortcrust pastry base, and is a French favourite for weddings. If making the choux pastry a day in advance, the buns can be crisped by heating in a preheated oven at 180°C,

350°F, Gas Mark 4, for 5 minutes. Cool before filling and assembling.

Choux Pastry
75g (3oz) butter
175ml (6 fl oz) water
100g (4oz) plain flour
Pinch of salt
3 beaten eggs

Filling
600ml (1 pint) double cream
30ml (2 tblsp) milk
30ml (2 tblsp) sifted icing sugar
30ml (2 tblsp) raspberry liqueur

Caramel
225g (8oz) granulated sugar
150ml (¼ pint) water

Sift the flour and salt together. Melt the butter in a heavy saucepan, with the water, and bring to the boil. Remove from heat. Add flour and salt mixture to the pan as soon as liquid has boiled. This should be carried out rapidly. Beat with a wooden spoon until glossy. The mixture should be the right consistency to form small balls at this stage. Turn out onto a plate and spread out to cool. Return it to the pan and gradually beat in the eggs. Fill a piping bag with the choux paste. Attach a 2cm (¾ inch) plain nozzle. Pipe the choux paste in small balls onto a greased baking sheet. Make sure they are well apart. Bake in the oven for 25 minutes until well risen and golden brown. They should be firm to touch. Pierce each bun to allow the steam to escape and return them to the oven for 2 minutes. Cool on a wire rack.

Filling
Whip half the cream with the milk, fold in the icing sugar and the raspberry liqueur. Whip the remaining cream and use half to form a mound in the centre of the serving plate or stand. With the other half, fill a piping bag fitted with a star nozzle and reserve. Use the raspberry cream to fill another piping bag fitted with a plain nozzle and fill each of the choux buns. Stick the choux buns round the cream mound so that it is completely covered and pipe rosettes between each bun using the plain cream.

For the Caramel
Melt the sugar gently in a saucepan with the water and boil until it turns brown and caramelizes. Cool until the caramel begins to thicken but not set and pour quickly, but gently, over the gâteau. Leave to set and chill for ½ hour before serving.

Loganberry Gâteau

PREPARATION TIME: 40 minutes

COOKING TIME: 35 minutes

OVEN TEMPERATURE: 190°C, 375°F, Gas Mark 5

4 eggs
125g (4oz) caster sugar
75g (3oz) plain flour
25g (1oz) melted butter
25g (1oz) cornflour
Grated rind of ½ lemon

Filling
450g (1lb) loganberries, fresh (or drained, if tinned)
90ml (6 tblsp) sherry
450ml (¾ pint) double cream, whipped
Finely-grated chocolate or chocolate vermicelli

Put the sugar, eggs and lemon rind in a basin over a pan of hot water and whisk until pale and thick. Remove from the heat and continue to whisk until cool. Sieve the flour and cornflour together. Fold the flour and melted butter into the mixture using a metal spoon. Bottom line and grease a 20cm (8 inch) square cake tin, fill with mixture and bake in the oven for 35 minutes. When cooked, turn out and cool on a wire rack. Cut the cake in half horizontally and sprinkle with sherry. Spread the bottom layer with whipped cream and reserve a little cream for decoration. Cover the cream with half the loganberries. Put the top layer of the sponge onto the loganberry filling and cover the sides of the cake with a thin layer of cream using a palette knife. Press the chocolate over the sides of the cake. Cover the top of the cake with a thin layer of cream and fill a

nylon piping bag fitted with a large nozzle with the remaining cream. Pipe a cream border round the top of the cake. Fill the top with the remaining loganberries.

Apricot Meringue

PREPARATION TIME: 30 minutes

COOKING TIME: 1 hour to 1 hour 15 minutes

OVEN TEMPERATURE: 140°C, 275°F, Gas Mark 1

6 egg whites
350g (12oz) caster sugar
450ml (15 fl oz) whipping cream, whipped
6 apricot halves, sliced

Line a baking sheet with non-stick paper. Whisk the egg whites in a clean, dry bowl until stiff. Continue to whisk and add the sugar, 15ml (1 tblsp) at a time, until the mixture is very stiff and glossy. Fit a large star nozzle to a piping bag and pipe 8 swirls onto the baking sheet. Bake in the oven for 1-1¼ hours until crisp and dry. Leave to cool and peel from the paper. Lay half the meringue swirls onto a presentation plate and fill a piping bag, fitted with a star nozzle, with the whipped cream. Pipe a line of cream onto each swirl and layer with slices of apricot. Pipe with cream again. Sandwich with another meringue swirl and pipe with cream around the edge of the top meringue and decorate the cream with further slices of apricot.

Facing page: Gateau St Honoré (top left), Minted Lime Gateau (top right) and Loganberry Gateau (bottom).

Black Forest Gâteau

PREPARATION TIME: 35 minutes

COOKING TIME: 40 minutes

OVEN TEMPERATURE: 190°C, 375°F, Gas Mark 5

3 eggs
125g (4oz) caster sugar
75g (3oz) plain flour
15g (½oz) cocoa powder

Filling

425g (15oz) tin black cherries, pitted
15ml (1 tblsp) arrowroot
30ml (2 tblsp) Kirsch
300ml (½ pint) double cream
Grated chocolate or chocolate flakes
   to decorate

Place the eggs and sugar in a basin and whisk over a saucepan of hot water until thick. Remove from the heat and continue to whisk until cool. Sieve the cocoa powder and flour together and gently fold into the mixture using a metal spoon. Grease and line the bottom of a 20cm (8 inch) cake tin. Pour the mixture into the tin and bake in the oven for 40 minutes. Turn out and cool on a wire rack.

Filling and Decoration

Drain the juice from the cherries into a pan and blend with a little arrowroot. Bring to boil and stir until it thickens. Add the cherries to the syrup and allow to cool. Cut the cake in half and sprinkle the base with a little Kirsch. Whip the cream and use it to fill a nylon piping bag fitted with a large star nozzle. Pipe a circle of cream into the border edge of the base cake. Fill with half the cherry mixture. Sprinkle the top of the cake with a little Kirsch and place on top of the filling. Spread a little cream on the sides of the gâteau and press the grated chocolate onto it, using a palette knife. Pipe swirls of cream on top of the gâteau and fill the centre with the remaining cherries. Sprinkle with a little chocolate.

Walnut and Banana Galette

PREPARATION TIME: 45 minutes

COOKING TIME: 25 minutes

OVEN TEMPERATURE: 180°C, 350°F, Gas Mark 4

175g (4oz) butter
175g (6oz) plain flour
125g (4oz) caster sugar
100g (4oz) chopped walnuts
Grated rind of ½ lemon

Filling and Decoration

300ml (½ pint) double cream
30ml (2 tblsp) icing sugar
4 bananas

Cream the butter, sugar and lemon rind until fluffy. Fold the flour in and knead it until you have a soft dough. Put the dough in a polythene bag and chill for ½ hour in the refrigerator. Grease and flour 3 baking sheets and mark an 18cm (7 inch) circle on each. To make the circles, use a saucepan lid as a guide. Divide the dough into 3 and place a piece of dough on each circle. Press it out until it fills the circle. Sprinkle the top of each circle with chopped walnuts and bake in the oven for 25 minutes. When cooked, allow to cool before turning onto a wire rack.

Filling and Decoration

Whip the cream and fold in the icing sugar. Slice the bananas and sprinkle them with a little lemon juice, which prevents them from discolouring. Sandwich the layers with some cream sprinkled with banana slices. Using a nylon piping bag filled with the remaining cream and fitted with a large star nozzle, pipe the decoration around the top of the galette and decorate with slices of banana. Allow the galette to stand for 30 minutes before serving.

Brandied Chestnut Roll

PREPARATION TIME: 35 minutes

COOKING TIME: 12 minutes for the base, 10 minutes for the filling

OVEN TEMPERATURE: 220°C, 425°F, Gas Mark 7

3 eggs
100g (4oz) caster sugar
30ml (2 tblsp) brandy
100g (4oz) plain flour

Filling

15ml (1 tblsp) caster sugar
300ml (½ pint) double cream
250g (8¾oz) tin chestnut purée
   (crème de marrons)
175g (6oz) plain chocolate
15g (½oz) butter
30ml (2 tblsp) brandy

Whisk the eggs and sugar until thick. Gently fold in the sieved flour and the brandy with a metal spoon. Line and grease (bottom only) a 23x33cm (9x13 inch) Swiss roll tin. Pour the mixture into the tin and bake in the oven for 12 minutes. Cover a clean, damp tea towel with a sheet of greaseproof paper. Sprinkle the paper with 15ml (1 tblsp) caster sugar. Turn the cake out onto the paper and remove the greaseproof paper used to line the tin. The edges of the cake will be crisp, so trim with a sharp knife. Roll up the cake by putting a clean sheet of greaseproof paper over the cake. Cool on a wire tray.

Filling

Whip the cream and sugar until stiff and stir half the cream into the chestnut purée. The chestnut purée mixture must be smooth before use. Gently unroll the cake and remove the greaseproof paper rolled with it. Spread the chestnut cream on the inner side of the cake and re-roll. Melt the chocolate in a bowl over a pan of hot water, adding the butter and brandy. Cover the cake completely with the chocolate mixture. Mark the chocolate-coated cake with a fork when half set. Pipe the whipped cream with a large nozzle into whirls on top of the cake.

Ginger Ice Cream Gâteau

PREPARATION TIME: 1 hour

COOKING TIME: 25 minutes

OVEN TEMPERATURE: 160°C, 325°F, Gas Mark 3

Ice Cream

150ml (5 fl oz) milk
1 egg
75g (3oz) caster sugar
50ml (2 fl oz) green ginger wine
300ml (½ pint) double cream

Almond Base

3 egg whites
150g (5oz) caster sugar
50g (2oz) cornflour
100g (4oz) ground almonds

Topping

150ml (5 fl oz) double cream
60ml (4 tblsp) apricot jam, sieved
3 pieces stem ginger, chopped
50g (2oz) toasted whole or flaked
   almonds

Ice Cream

Put the milk, egg and sugar into a basin over a pan of hot water. Stir continuously until the custard mixture begins to thicken. When it will coat the back of the spoon, remove it and let it cool. Stir in the ginger wine and cream. Pour into a rigid, shallow freezer container and partially freeze. When the ice cream is partially frozen, remove from the freezer and pour into a bowl. Whisk until smooth and creamy. Line a 20cm (8 inch) sandwich tin with cling film and pour in the ice cream. Return to the freezer until frozen.

Almond Base

Whisk the egg whites in a clean bowl until they are stiff. Add the sugar and whisk again. Gently fold in the cornflour and ground almonds. Line the bottom of a baking tray. Fill a nylon piping bag fitted with a 1cm (½ inch) nozzle with some of the almond mixture. Spread the mixture in a 20cm (8 inch) circle and smooth evenly. Bake in the oven for 25 minutes. Place the almond base on a flat plate. Carefully lift the ice cream out of the tin and peel off the cling film. Place the ice cream on the almond base.

For the Topping

Whip the cream, fold in the jam, stem ginger and almonds and spread over the ice cream.

Brandied Chestnut Roll (left), Walnut and
Banana Galette (below) and Black Forest
Gâteau (bottom).

Peach and Almond Gâteau

PREPARATION TIME: 60 minutes

COOKING TIME: 60 minutes for cake, 20 minutes for confectioner's custard

OVEN TEMPERATURE: 180°C, 350°F, Gas Mark 4

4 eggs, separated
100g (4oz) caster sugar
100g (4oz) self-raising flour
30ml (2 tblsp) corn oil
45ml (3 tblsp) boiling water
5ml (1 tsp) almond essence

Filling
30ml (2 tblsp) apricot jam, warmed

Confectioner's Custard
3 egg yolks
50g (2oz) caster sugar
25g (1oz) plain flour
300ml (½ pint) milk
25g (1oz) butter
10ml (1 dsp) sherry

To Decorate
300ml (½ pint) double cream
50g (2oz) flaked almonds, toasted
410g (14½oz) tin sliced peaches, drained

Grease and line a 20cm (8 inch) loose-bottomed, deep cake tin. Place the egg yolks, sugar, flour, oil, water and almond essence in a bowl and beat for 2 minutes with a wooden spoon. Stiffly whisk the egg whites and fold into the cake mixture using a metal spoon. Pour the mixture into a prepared tin and cook in the oven for about 60 minutes until well risen. Remove cake from tin and cool on a wire rack. Remove paper when cake is cold.

For the Confectioner's Custard
Put egg yolks in a bowl and beat until smooth and creamy. Stir in the flour and mix well. Heat the milk until hot, but not boiling, and stir into the egg mixture. Return the mixture to the pan and stir, bringing it gently to the boil. Remove from the heat and beat in the butter and the sherry. Pour into a bowl, stirring occasionally to prevent a skin forming.

Assembling the Gâteau
Cut the cake into 3 layers, placing the bottom layer on a serving plate. Spread the cake with 15ml (1 tblsp) of jam and half the confectioner's custard. Place the second layer on top and spread

with the remaining jam and custard. Put the top of the cake onto the filling. Spread the cake with half the cream and arrange the peaches on the top. Fit a piping bag with a medium star nozzle and pipe the remaining cream to decorate the gâteau. Sprinkle on the toasted almonds.

Chocolate Torte

PREPARATION TIME: 35 minutes

COOKING TIME: 1 hour 30 minutes

OVEN TEMPERATURE: 150°C, 300°F, Gas Mark 2

175g (6oz) plain chocolate
15ml (1 tblsp) strong black coffee
175g (6oz) butter
175g (6oz) caster sugar
4 eggs, separated
150g (5oz) self-raising flour

Filling and Icing
Cherry jam
175g (6oz) plain chocolate
30ml (2 tblsp) strong black coffee
175g (6oz) icing sugar
150ml (5 fl oz) double cream or 100g (4oz) chocolate shavings
410g (14½oz) tinned black cherries, pitted

Melt the chocolate and coffee over a basin of hot water. Allow it to cool. Cream the butter and sugar together until light and fluffy. Slowly beat in the egg yolks and the cooled chocolate mixture. Fold in the flour using a metal spoon. Whisk the egg whites in a clean, dry bowl until stiff, then fold into the mixture. Line and grease the base of a 20cm (8 inch) cake tin and bake in the oven for 1½ hours. Allow the cake to cool in the tin for 10 minutes before turning onto a wire rack. Cut the cake horizontally and sandwich together with the cherry jam. Melt the chocolate and coffee for the icing in a basin over a saucepan of hot water and remove from the heat. Beat in the icing sugar. Pour the chocolate icing over the cake, working it over the sides of the cake with a palette knife. When set, decorate with either the whipped cream or chocolate shavings and drained cherries.

Avocado Cheesecake

PREPARATION TIME: 30 minutes plus chilling

Biscuit Base
225g (8oz) chocolate digestive biscuits
75g (3oz) butter, melted

Filling
2 ripe avocado pears
100g (4oz) cream cheese
75g (3oz) caster sugar
Juice of ½ a lemon
Grated rind of 1 lemon
10ml (2 tsp) gelatine powder
2 egg whites
150ml (5 fl oz) double cream, whipped

Decoration
150ml (5 fl oz) double cream, whipped

Crush the biscuits into fine crumbs and stir in the melted butter. Use the mixture to line a 19cm (7½ inch) springform tin. Press it down to line the base and the sides. Chill well.

For the Filling
Peel and stone the avocados and save a few slices for decoration. Put the remainder into a basin and mash well. Mix in the lemon juice and grated rind, cream cheese and sugar. Beat until smooth. Dissolve the gelatine in 30ml (2 tblsp) of hot water and stir into the mixture. Whisk the egg whites in a clean, dry bowl and fold into the mixture with the whipped cream. Pour onto a prepared biscuit base and chill thoroughly until set.

To Decorate
Carefully remove the cheesecake from the tin. Fill a nylon piping bag, fitted with a star nozzle, with the cream reserved for decoration. Pipe a border of cream round the edge of the cake. Decorate with the avocado slices.
NB: sprinkle the avocado with lemon juice to prevent it from discolouring. This is useful when reserving the slices for decoration.

This page: Chocolate Torte (top) and Apricot Meringue (bottom).

Facing page: Avocado Cheesecake (top), Ginger Ice Cream Gâteau (centre left) and Peach and Almond Gâteau (bottom).

Index